Bring Life
into Learning

Bring Life into Learning

Create a Lasting Literacy

Donald H. Graves

HEINEMANN
Portsmouth, NH

Heinemann
A division of Reed Elsevier Inc.
361 Hanover Street
Portsmouth, NH 03801–3912
http://www.heinemann.com

Offices and agents throughout the world

The author and publisher wish to thank those who have generously given permission to reprint borrowed material:

Excerpt from *The Human Experience* by the Quaker US/USSR Committee. Copyright © 1989 by the Quaker US/USSR Committee. Reprinted by permission of Alfred A. Knopf Inc.

Excerpt from *The Game* by Ken Dryden. Copyright © Ken Dryden 1983, 1993. Reprinted by permission of Macmillan Canada and the Author.

Library of Congress Cataloging-in-Publication Data
CIP is on file with the Library of Congress.
ISBN: 0-325-00170-7

Editor: Lois Bridges
Production: Vicki Kasabian
Cover design: Michael Leary Design
Manufacturing: Louise Richardson

Printed in the United States of America on acid-free paper
03 02 01 00 99   DA   1 2 3 4 5

To the editorial and production staff at Heinemann,
who bring life to teachers

Contents

Acknowledgments

Writing a book is a long journey and many people help along the way. Before I had written one line, I explored the idea of focusing on character in stories and on people in the disciplines with Jane Hansen, Lois Bridges, and Leigh Peake. I also ran the idea by Camille Allen. All were encouraging.

I thank the countless teachers around the country who responded to the first four chapters in various workshops.

Early in my draft, I consulted with Maura Sullivan from the marketing department at Heinemann about my blurb and the direction of this book. Her marketing texts lifted my sights for the book at hand. She walked with me with wry humor and grace through the entire book.

I received much help for the chapters on history, art, and science (whatever errors may appear in the text are my own). Nancie Atwell listened to my first chapters and pointed me to Joy Hakim's history texts. Regie Routman read portions of the text and has been a daily correspondent through much of the writing. Bill Varner of Heinemann supplied professional materials on history curriculum and was an excellent critic in reviewing my history chapters. Wendy Saul and Fred Allen were especially helpful with the science chapters and reoriented my inaccurate assumptions about "doing" science. Rob Richardson, my regular Wednesday noon walking companion, was a constant resource, and I am grateful for both his friendship and our far-ranging professional discussions.

Karen Ernst was an especially helpful reader. Her critical comments about my first chapter and balance at various points sharpened the text.

I am grateful to each of the three people who granted me interviews: Hal Bridges, Juliette Hamelecourt, and Bruce Hill.

Donald Murray is always there for consultation about writing and about life in general. We discuss our mutual technological toys as we seek to remain in tune with changes in cyberspace, the Red Sox, Celtics, and sports in general.

My wife, Betty, has listened to my readings of the entire book and always reads my texts critically. "Sounds good," she says, "now let me read it." I find that I don't write well when she is away for a day. I don't seem to take the necessary risks unless I know I can run downstairs to share a text with her.

Lois Bridges, my editor, and I have been in daily contact since the genesis of the book. Both her encouragement and her critical reading make writing a joy and a challenge. Lois is passionate on behalf of teachers and children. How easy it is to write in the morning when Lois says, "Let's have more of this!"

I am grateful to Vicki Kasabian, the production editor at Heinemann who has led me capably through the last details of bringing the book to fruition.

Finally, this book is dedicated to the people at Heinemann. We have grown together. I have enjoyed the best of editors over the years: Philippa Stratton, Toby Gordon, and Lois Bridges. More recently, the company has moved to newer levels of excellence under the leadership of Mike Gibbons and Leigh Peake. Heinemann has made it possible for teachers to publish, to bring a new level of professionalism to teaching. It has been a pioneer, and now many other publishers have followed its example of excellence.

1

Let's Bring People Back into the Curriculum

We live in a culture that worships speed. Spend an hour watching television. Listen to the advertisements that promise *instant* relief, more rapid computer processing, "quick and easy" financing, the fastest acceleration in a new car, or one-minute microwave dinners. Pay particular attention to the plots of sitcoms, adventure stories, or police dramas with their jump-cut action and snappy lines. How often do you encounter well-developed people or gain any understanding of why they make the choices they do?

Schools Don't Escape

Our schools don't escape the influence of our high-speed culture. Teachers face increasingly inflated school curricula that leave them with less time to teach. More and more, they are forced to cover prescribed materials rather than ideas or experiences with more enduring lessons. Teachers and children sprint through the day, busy from beginning to end, pressured as well by the demands of the standardized tests children will be required to take. Real learning, learning that lasts, is a major casualty.

Witness the teaching of reading. When the class discusses stories, children learn to focus on plot, on "what happened," which is partly developmental but also partly cultural. But the plot can only be fully understood through the characters and their individual passions, needs, and desires. There are rarely simple explanations for characters' motivations or class time enough to consider them. Teacher guidebooks accompanying reading series, workbooks, and small group discussions emphasize plot, as do standardized tests, which supply paragraphs for children to read and a list of questions to answer. Such approaches, however, do not get at the heart of what reading and interpreting a text are all about. The questions usually consider only setting, the order of events, and who the main characters are.

Writing also suffers in the high-speed school culture. If children's fiction writing is to move beyond plot, teachers need to show them how to portray rounded characters. Good teaching that focuses on character can have a dramatic affect on children's writing. Their writing gains depth and their discussions of the fiction they are reading borrows from their own experience as writers.

When professional writers discuss their fiction, questions about their characters are often foremost: "From all that we know about Antoine so far, do you really think he'd stoop to petty thievery?" The author has to supply enough evidence about what sort of person Antoine is to make petty thievery plausible. Plot doesn't just happen.

Although it is common in literary circles to discuss fictional characters in relation to plot, I want to broaden the discussion to include other areas of the curriculum. Historic events happen because people make them happen. Scientific breakthroughs are made because people observe, formulate, and test hypotheses, and publish their results. Artists see the world in unique ways and share their vision with the rest of us. Bypass people and you bypass learning.

People in History

Teaching often focuses on the forces of history and neglects the people who put those forces in motion. The American colonies didn't suddenly break away from England; England's economic demands gradually conflicted with those of the colonists, until force was required to resolve the standoff. History is the story of people wrestling with events, but events are the result of people acting separately or corporately.

Thomas Jefferson and John Adams, two very different personalities, met with other like-minded men in Philadelphia to hammer out the Declaration of Independence: Jefferson, the wealthy Virginian, rides with his entourage through fruit trees in blossom. John Adams leaves his home in Quincy, Massachusetts, in the spring snows of New England and, with one companion, spends three weeks on horseback to reach Philadelphia, where he arrives ready to bring about the

Declaration through the sheer force of personality and logic. All the signers know that if they are captured, they will be hanged, or worse, drawn and quartered. With thirty thousand British troops in the New York area, only two day's march from Philadelphia, their danger is real. Abraham Lincoln searches desperately for a general who wants to fight. As a man of peace, he struggles because he knows so many young men will die on both sides.

Leave out the human story and history cannot be properly understood. Children will *learn* to dislike it. It takes real, multidimensional characters to engage children in the drama of history, and in a democracy it is especially important that future citizens feel a sense of engagement in the events of the past. Simply learning dates, names, places, or the causes of the Civil War provides little sense of immediacy; it ignores the human passions and the decision making behind the conflict.

I want children to know that those who have come before them have made choices both good and bad, sometimes under very difficult conditions. Through Lincoln's letters and notes, for example, they can see how he regarded his generals or the members of his cabinet. By reading and thinking about such matters they begin to consider how they might proceed under similar circumstances and to understand some of the complexities of leadership.

The Writer-Scientist

A few years ago I wrote an article for *Dragon Fly*, a magazine for children and teachers published by the National Science Foundation. I wanted to give them a glimpse into the world of field science and show its parallels with writing. Here is how I began the article:

> My steps sound like I walk on Rice Krispies as I pass through the trails in our woodland. We've had a dry spring, summer and fall. Drought has a certain sound to it. Squirrels running through leaves sound like antelopes; a moose steps on a fallen branch and the snap echoes through the hemlocks like a rifle shot. Like a scientist I am in a constant state of composition. I observe details, formulate hypotheses, and connect one shard of information with another.

This will not be a good fall for our black bears. Their natural forage in September and October is beechnuts and acorns. But the drought has taken its toll on that food supply. Apple growers complain about bears who raid their orchards to fill their stomachs. But the apples won't provide the vital fat bears take in from the nuts required for winter hibernation, but especially to suckle their young born in January. If the pregnant sow doesn't have enough fat by the end of the fall season, her body automatically aborts the fetus. My trail on inquiry begins with the sounds of drought, moves to the effect of drought on trees and the lack of nuts, and ends with the sow's pregnancy.

There is little difference between the thinking of the writer and scientist. Both observe phenomena and formulate hypotheses to connect the meaning of events. They are fascinated by data that do not fit the norm. Exception is the root of wonder; the unexplained, the source of further inquiry, and unease is a sign of further exploration into the unknown.

We need to visit with people in science and be privy to their thinking. Our children need to try on the lenses of the scientist when they look at the world.

Point of View and the Law of Polarity

Studying people brings up the question of *point of view*. One person's passions and wishes soon encounter others. Indeed, other passions often arise from countervailing viewpoints. Writers of fiction call this *the law of polarity* (Carroll 1996). For example, a twelve-year-old boy loses his father at sea. The boy wants to live up to his father's ideals, yet he must grow up to be his own person. The constant struggle within surfaces in his inconsistent dealings with other people. At the same time, his mother makes him feel confined and contained, a child wanting to be a man.

Artists try to bend the poles, to move the opposing forces toward understanding, but the result is often paradox: Goya places innocence and brutality side by side in his painting of an execution. Life leaps the gap between God's finger and man's reach in Michaelangelo's painting of creation on the Sistine Chapel ceiling. In John Gardiner's *Stone*

Fox, Little Willie's grandfather is bedridden and the boy must perform a man's work to save the farm. Great obstacles must be overcome and the passion to succeed pulls us along. In the course of a lifetime we live out one paradox after another. The minute one thing is settled, new questions, new problems arise. The poles may bend, but they never come together.

It is the human condition that there is rarely a full resolution between points of view. We teach, however, as if information is static. But human beings are messy and unpredictable, as dangerous as they are delightful. Our quest to be gods, to be omnipotent, leads us to climb Mt. Everest, write novels, sculpt a *David*, and compose symphonies, but it can also lead us to murder and to instigate pogroms. We find ourselves the source of hilarious comedy and heart-rending tragedy. To ignore our fellow human beings is to miss out on the greatest journey of all, that of becoming human ourselves.

Our colleagues in teaching are weary. We have been derailed from this very important journey. Legislative, administrative, and public distrust leads us to emphasize methods and materials and to ignore our own best judgments. Curriculum inflation and constant classroom interruptions tear at the vital time we need to achieve greater depth in our teaching and effective human engagement with our children. To an already impossible situation, one external assessment after another is added.

When I enter the teacher's room in almost any school in the country and ask, "Is anyone tired?," the response is a unanimous "yes." Teachers feel drained and dispirited not from hard work but from the weight of distrust heaped on them by people who do not know what it means to teach. The growing impersonality of human relations in education creates a faceless curriculum. In turn, we observe with growing alarm the dull, weary edges of our own personalities.

It is time to begin to renew ourselves and our teaching. We need to bring a new sense of adventure to our own learning and to our teaching. Let's rethink our curriculum and focus on the lives of historical figures, artists, and scientists. We'll take the journey together and learn through practical teaching experiments that I call ACTIONS. ACTIONS are practices that allow you to gain a greater understanding of a subject by taking you through a series of first-hand experiences. I usually do the ACTIONS right along with you to introduce you to the experience. It is in the doing, not in the reading, that you will experience the energy in this approach to curriculum. These experiments should give us an opportunity to reconsider the kind of learning that lasts and to become reacquainted with people across the disciplines. First we will write about people by creating fictional characters, then examine the characters in our reading, and finally, explore how we can learn through the minds of people in history, science, and the arts.

As important as this study may be, however, remember that you are still the most important person your students will encounter this year.

2

A Workshop on People

"Frances is just plain disorganized." My friend's comment hangs heavy in the air like a dark cloud. "Now, about the party we'll be having next Friday." She moves on to other plans, but her first statement lingers in the room.

One of my pet peeves in conversation and in writing is the assertion of a statement or a conclusion with no supporting evidence. Frances may well be disorganized, but my friend has given me no evidence to allow me to come to my own conclusion. I need to know more about Frances. I especially need to see her in action, to have a graphic example of her disorganization. Writers speak of showing versus telling. Let me demonstrate what I mean ("telling" will be in regular type, "showing" in italic):

Frances is disorganized. *The other day I saw her dive into her purse to hunt for a list. She tossed scrap pieces of paper, credit cards, keys, and a date book onto the table. "Oh, it must be in here somewhere," she moaned. "You'd think I'd take a moment to clean this thing out but I never seem to."*

"Frances is disorganized" is the statement or conclusion. The words in italic illustrate Frances' apparent disorganization. We see the scattered items (nouns) she tosses onto the table: scrap pieces of paper, credit cards, keys, and date book. William Carlos Williams says, "No ideas but in things." The nouns are the stuff of showing as is the verb "tosses," which suggests disorganization (*placed* would convey a different sense).

ACTION: *Choose a person you know well and list the ways in which she reveals herself.*

I am going to choose my father, who passed away a year ago, as an example. My list reflects my image of him about five years ago, when he was eighty-seven, just after my mother passed away.

- Grip—Dad had a thorny grip from hours of weeding.
- Missing middle finger on right hand—lost in a rototiller accident.
- Dirt under fingernails—working in the garden. Even before he retired as a Supt. of Schools, he rarely attended to his nails.
- Baseball cap—wore this from spring through fall. He'd always liked baseball.
- Mud and dirt on shoes.
- Hair standing up on head—combed it under protest.
- Holding fist of gladiola spikes—hybridized glads for fifty years.
- His reading: always sports page, New England Glad society journal, seed catalogs, Bridgewater Alumni news, *Sporting News*, *Sports Illustrated*.
- Shirt, usually untucked.
- Answers telephone by second ring. Cryptic language. "Yup, no, we can take care of that. Have you attended to what you'll need." Businesslike language, flowers under "grow lights," African violets, seedlings.
- Odor: smelling of fertilizer and sweat.
- Favorite chair facing television set.
- Handwriting—irregular, angular script suggesting great hurry.
- Dirty glasses.
- Walks with a limp as if feet, legs, or hips hurt.
- Thick wallet in rear left pocket.
- Shaves in a hurry—cuts self.
- Typical sentences and phrases spoken in slightly nasal tone:
  See the game last night?
  What time did you leave?
  Need any money?
  This drought is killing the garden.
  We've had so much rain the bulbs will rot in the ground.
  The dog been fed yet?
  Gonna have a cup of coffee.
  Can't find my . . .
  Better leave now or you'll get stuck in traffic.
  Paper hasn't come yet.
- Description: *Shoulders up:* baseball cap, hair poking beneath cap, brown eyes behind dirty glasses, snub nose, large ears, white gray

hair, thrust jaw. *Shoulders down*: 175 pounds, short-sleeved shirt, paunch, belt pulled tight separating stomach from hips and legs.

As I read over my list I notice that the picture I've created is rather static. I've concentrated on nouns and left out verbs. I'll try another list.

- Jams wallet back into his pocket.
- Jumps in seat when telephone rings.
- Swallows loudly while drinking coffee.
- Tugs at weeds.
- Turns quickly to go out the screen door into the garden.
- Shuffles across the lawn.
- Digs through magazines until he finds the one he wants, scatters others on floor.
- Tears off shirt when undressing, often popping buttons.
- Holds a hug when hugging.

After you have completed your list, set it aside. Return to it another day and read it aloud to see if there are other items you can add. Writing is in itself an act of memory. The words on your list will trigger others as images of the person you know slowly emerge.

ACTION: *Write a short paragraph about the person you have described showing that person in a familiar situation.*

I recall Dad at eighty-seven walking up to the house from the garden, a very familiar memory. As I write I am going to disregard the lists I composed earlier. Listing my father's attributes gave my memory a good stir. Now I'll do a rapid sketch and see what happens (once again, the "showing" sentences are in italic):

> "Got some good seedlings this morning," Dad says as he *shuffles across the wet morning grass. He is clutching a fist of four glad spikes in his right hand.* Mother always moaned about Dad wearing his good clothes into the garden and this day he's done it again. *Mud spots mark his knees and the toes of his shoes. The middle button on what used to be a Sunday shirt is missing. The brim of his baseball cap has a slight dent where he's tugged the hat to his head for the last three summers.* "One of these might amount to

something, especially this peach-colored one," *he says, separating it from the others, the slight, shy smile of pride daring to touch his mouth.*

I have tried to record essential aspects of my father in this one instant using the same approach a cartoonist uses: his complete disregard for clothing, his love of gladioluses, which certainly took primacy over personal appearance. When something was very good, a slight smile might reach his mouth. Dad wasn't one to praise himself, but sometimes a new seedling, one of his best crosses, would bring him close to admitting that he'd done something special.

ACTION: *Take ten minutes to do a quick written sketch of a person you do not know.*

I often do a mental version of this exercise in an airport while waiting for my flight. I'll spot someone several aisles away and try to create a story about that person, to imagine where their lives are headed. I may do the same at a concert or a baseball game, sitting in a library, a restaurant, or a hospital waiting room, at a church service, or even observing children on the playground. Here is an example of how I go about this exercise.

- How do they present themselves to the world? (Grooming, clothing—care, don't care?)
- What are they carrying? (Bundles, book, packages, briefcase.)
- If eating, what are they eating?
- If talking, are they the listener? the storyteller? the dominant person in dyad or triad? Do they use their hands to accent their speech? Do they sit close, lean in, sit erect, sit, or stand back? Do they make eye contact?
- Are they curious about their surroundings? Do they observe, interact, or depart into a book or their own thoughts?
- If you are close enough to hear conversation, listen for tone of voice, accent, choice of words.

Sketch in these categories for yourself and then write a one-paragraph piece *showing* what you have observed about the person. Since you don't know the person, give him or her a name. It will help you to pull the details together.

After I had observed someone at another restaurant table one evening, I wrote the following paragraph:

Neil McGinnis leaned into conversation the way he ran his business, all chin, mouth, and chest. A pencil mustache contrasted sharply with his L. L. Bean plaid shirt. "City guy trying to look country," I figured. Fifteen strands of hair were strategically combed across his bald pate. A young woman many years his junior leaned back in her seat as McGinnis stabbed the air with a fork to accentuate his main points.

Once again, I have chosen a few essential elements to bring out my subject's character: he is pushy, even overpowering. His pencil mustache seems out of place in the context of his clothing. Perhaps he believes no one will notice. He doesn't realize how transparent he is to others.

Final Reflection

In this chapter we have practiced observing people and composing brief descriptions of friends and strangers. Writers always know far more than they can ever put on paper, so they choose only essential details. Readers use these details as evidence in understanding the characters' actions and the story's meaning. In Chapter 3 we will learn more about ourselves as readers. We'll try ACTIONS that take us through a reading selection and a close examination of the characters in a story.

3

Learning to Read Characters

When I read, I always bring my emotions with me. I read in order to understand, but I also read to engage with an author, a character, or a historical figure. I want to feel what they feel, to sense their deepest longings. In short, I read to meet people. They, in turn, help me to understand myself. People I meet on the page can be just as ornery or delightful as people I meet on the street. Some I like, some I don't; some I detest, but some I find fascinating.

As an undergraduate I was a little humorless when I read novels. I was on a quest to understand life, and I worked hard to put together a personal philosophy which I could live by. I remember a course on the English novel that took me through Thackeray, Austen, Bennett, and Dickens. The professor laughed through *Vanity Fair,* but too much of the humor derived from the nuances of class and the manners and manipulations associated with one's "station." I simply couldn't engage with the characters and my prejudice affected the quality of my reading: my conclusions about the characters were often at odds with those of my fellow students.

I had a different experience reading the novels of Tolstoy, Dostoevsky, Turgenev, Gogol, and Chekhov. Their characters confronted philosophical questions. They wrestled with pacifism, justifiable homicide, inheritance, infidelity, love, and marriage. Many of the English characters struggled with the same wants but didn't seem to reflect on them in the same way. I am still trying to distinguish the differences in effect between the English and Russian authors. The Russians provided a solid foundation for thinking about basic life issues. I was soon to be drafted to fight in the Korean War, and Tolstoy's portrayal of pacifism in *War and Peace* in the character Pierre Bezhukov widened the frame of discussion for me. Prince Andrew Bolkonsky in the same novel reflected the futility of war. I often found myself thinking about subjects that seemed far removed from Russia or characters: "Will I marry? What is love? What will become of me? Is it right to kill?" Sometimes I became more interested in my own thoughts than in the assigned material, but I found myself in the midst of text-related class discussions when I wanted to explore deeper thoughts inspired by the material.

Recently, in conducting a workshop on understanding and portraying characters, I asked the group to read "The Boy and the Moose," which follows. Read it now with this question in mind: "What do these people want?"

The Boy and the Moose

A loud snap echoed through the tall hemlocks bordering the swamp at the base of Iron Mountain. Edney Sawkins slowly turned his head to the left and in the direction of the noise. The loudness of the snap could only mean one thing: his friend, the bull moose, was on his way to an afternoon feast in the bog. No human could step on a branch and produce the loud crack, not even if one of the big loggers deliberately cracked a two-inch branch across his knee.

Quite suddenly the moose emerged from the thicket of swamp maples beneath the hemlocks and at the edge of the bog. He stood, eyes blinking, adjusting to the bright sun that greeted him in the open space of the swamp. "Next he'll turn and look at me," Edney whispered to himself. Slowly, as predicted, the giant head of the moose turned to stare directly at the boy. Edney took in the sad, blinking eyes, the great rack of antlers, some six feet across, the long snout of a nose shaped like a violin case, and the beard hanging beneath his jaw.

Edney first met his moose toward the end June. The relief as well as the pain of the last day at school sent him to his woods to be alone. He remembered the loneliness of the office that last day when he sat at a table with the school people and his parents. Edney could only remember fragments of Mr. Huckaby's words delivered in a monotone and sounding like the usual gobbledygook, "Another school . . . deal with his problem . . . more help there." He'd looked that pastey-faced counselor dead in the eye. He was one of those sweet-talking school men with thick lips who dripped words like he was a real doctor or something. Next he looked at his mother who carried sorrow in her eyes and hands beneath the table that he knew were wringing and clinging to each other in that moment as if to let go she'd lose hold of life itself. She was his only hope to say something on his behalf. She simply said, "Whatever's best for Edney."

Dad just sat there, silent like a clumsy black bear not made for sitting on real chairs. He leaned forward, staring straight ahead and not at Edney. Thick black eyebrows accented deep, brooding brown eyes. At least today he'd shaved and put on a clean plaid shirt, the one he usually wore when out logging with the men. The District psychologist added the final line with a smile, "I'm sure this will work out for the best for everyone."

Edney pounded the table and screamed at everyone present, "You can't make me go. I'm not going and that's final." He liked the feel of hot tears that usually accompanied these familiar outbursts. But he couldn't get the adults angry. They sat there as if they expected him to shout.

He screamed at his mother when he got home. "Why are you sending me away to that dumb school? Just because I can't read and get mad. Anyway, it's all junk and I won't go." Mother sat there wringing her hands again. "We don't know how to help you, Edney. This ought to work for the best. Everyone at school wants the best for you. I know you don't understand now but someday you will."

He'd sassed her back pushing hard to get her angry. "You want me gone? Well, I'll go and I'm gettin' out o' here, startin' now!" He stormed out the back door glancing back to see if his mother was angry. Instead, her hands just got tighter and she was more quiet than ever.

Edney walked down the long hill behind the house, into the hemlocks, and down his favorite trail to the bog. The peace of the bog clearing usually cooled him after a good row. He sat on a stump thinking, "I'll sit here 'til dark and maybe they'll try to find me." He picked another stump with a smooth surface and next to a boulder, leaned back, closed his eyes and dozed off.

He was awakened from his nap by heavy breathing, breathing that sounded like some factory machine. He looked up and not twenty feet from him was the giant moose that stood a good seven feet high at the shoulder. Edney held his breath as he watched the moose wade into the swamp. For nearly an hour and a half he watched the animal wade up to its shoulders, then lower his head until it disappeared and rise with grass and watercress dangling from the sides of the long jaw, while streams of water poured down from his beard creating his own private waterfall.

Several times a week in late afternoon Edney returned to his favorite stump just when the sun dipped behind Iron Mountain. Although the moose went through his usual eating routines, Edney noticed that as the summer wore on his friend walked closer to him, even turned his head more often to give him a dreamy stare. Edney translated the look to, "Glad you showed up. Could always use a little company."

As the end of August approached, a heavy, cold feeling began to grow in his stomach at the prospect of leaving home, his beloved woods, and new friend, the moose. The weight turned from a general coldness to solid lead at dinner one night when his father announced with unusual glee that he'd been selected by the moose lottery. "Yup, I'm one of 5000 hunters selected to get me a moose. This winter, by thunder, we're goin' to have a full freezer of meat. Now I've got about six weeks to start checkin' moose habits around here so's when the season opens I've got me the one I want."

ACTION: *Consider each of the characters in "The Boy and the Moose."*

As an option, try this ACTION with a partner. Compare and contrast your understanding of the characters. Try this ACTION by following these steps in the recommended sequence.

1. Without looking back at the text, note what you think each of the following characters in the story *wants:* Edney, father, mother, moose, Mr. Huckaby.

Be sure to consider both the short- and the long-term desires each might have. For example, in the short term Mr. Huckaby wants Mr. and Mrs. Sawkins to agree with the school's recommendation that Edney be placed in a special school. In the long term, Mr. Huckaby probably wants to be regarded as a competent professional who can handle tough situations with a troubled student.

2. Now turn back to the story and reread it. As you read, try to identify the characters' internal and external conflicts.

15

Edney, for example, doesn't want to go away to school, but he also doesn't want anything to happen to the moose.

3. Which struggles interest you the most? The least? Why?

You may find it useful to consider which of the characters engages you the most. Although Edney receives more attention in the text, you may find yourself viewing the story through his mother's eyes. Some children, on the other hand, may identify more with the moose than with the counselor, Mr. Huckaby.

4. Try to recall any thoughts elicited by the text that have no connection to the actual story.

Reading often launches us into productive thinking quite unrelated to the text at hand. Here, for example, one reader might begin to plan a hike into the woods to establish a blind for observing wildlife. Another might recall a student with an emotional disability. For parents, the story could serve as a reminder of the struggles of one of their children. In reading, comprehension and interpretation are important, but children may not realize that good readers also value the thinking a text inspires, even if it is only peripherally related. Reading is a path to mindful living and continued learning. A text may point a reader in a new or untried direction.

5. Call the partner who has agreed to carry out this ACTION with you. Compare what you have discovered about yourselves as readers, and your thinking about the story, in the first four steps.

Remember that readers differ in their preferences, in their understanding of characters, and especially in the personal associations triggered by a text that can lead to meaningful thinking.

Final Reflection

When I read I try to climb inside the text, I become the characters and share in the unfolding of events. We need to help our students deepen their reading experiences, especially in terms of the people they encounter in fiction, biography and autobiography, and in nonfiction writing in the disciplines. When children begin to understand how to "read" people, they interpret the world more effectively. At the same time, they see themselves and their classmates from different perspectives.

4

A Reading and Writing Workshop on Character

Lola Mapes ushered me into her fourth-grade classroom in West Des Moines, Iowa. A technician with a video camera followed close behind. Moments before, in the teacher's room, Lola had commented that the stories the children were writing were making her ill: "So much violence, and the plots don't seem to be going anywhere."

"Perhaps I could demonstrate a way to help them understand the process of writing fiction."

"Be my guest," Lola answered, and we headed down the hallway to meet the children as they came in from recess.

The workshop I was about to introduce was one I'd been experimenting with in New Hampshire classrooms. My objective was to help children write a story together. They would come up with content and I would show them the kinds of questions writers ask themselves in order to produce a plausible story. What follows are excerpts from the video recording interspersed with my commentary in italic.

Don: All right, children, I'd like you to come over with me and sit on the rug. Pack in real tight because we're going to create a story together, one you choose, and I'll help you to do it by asking you some questions. You'll want to say things and I need to see everyone. Real tight now.

The setting is much the same as the one I use for telling or reading stories. I don't want to miss anyone. Above all, I want good eye contact so I can judge the children's involvement and spot those who may be on the verge of saying something but are holding back.

Don: We're going to create a story together. But first I need some suggestions on what you'd like the story to be about. I'll take three suggestions. Then you can vote on the one you wish to use. Let's have a show of hands with suggestions. Yes?

Child: Let's have it be about someone lost on an island all alone.

Don: OK, that's one, let's have another. Yes?

Child: How about someone gets kidnapped and there might be a murder?

Don: OK, now we have two: someone lost and a kidnapping. We need one more. Yes?

Child: A mother and father are in an argument and there's going to be a divorce.

Don: All right, that's three.

Inwardly I gasp, but I ask for a show of hands on each of the three. All vote for the third, the mother and father in an argument; not even the child who has suggested kidnapped votes for his own. Notice that I have solicited plot suggestions. I begin there because most children focus on plot. It is the easiest place for them to enter into the workshop. My task will be to <u>lead them back to character</u>, to ask questions that will help them become interested in the people in the story.

Don: You say there's a mother and a father. That means, I guess, that there are children. First we need to give the mother and father names, along with a last name. The names you choose cannot be the names of anyone here in this class or in the entire school. The names have to be new.

I learned the hard way in an earlier workshop in New Hampshire. I looked over at a boy and saw tears. Unknown to me, the children had chosen his name, and the unfolding story embarrassed him. I immediately ended that workshop. Names are important to establish character. The act of naming is a powerful tool in the hands of any author.

Child: How about John and Barbara Dunderlin?

Don: Are you all sure that isn't the name of anyone around here? (*I look at this teacher for confirmation.*) All right, class, do you agree with this choice?

During the workshop I always ask the children if they agree with a suggestion. If there is a difference of opinion I consider whether a discussion would

19

be significant to learning about fiction. The class decides that there are two children, a boy and a girl. The boy (Tim) is about ten years of age and the girl (Jennie) about eight.

Don: We need to know about John Dunderlin. What's he like around the house? Yes?
Child: He just sits there and says, "I'm tired."
Child: He, like, watches TV and stares at the wall.
Don: OK, he seems to be tired and stares at the wall. Does that seem right to you? (*They all agree.*) OK, does he have an occupation? Yes?
Child: He's a doctor. (*All agree to this.*)
Don: OK, one more. Yes?
Child: He says he's always on call, but really he has a girlfriend in another town. *All heads go up and down on this one. I feel as if I am running a session in group therapy.*
Don: That's enough about Dad. Tell me about the mother. What's she like around the house? Yes?
Child: She's easygoing.
Child: And she listens to the kids.
Don: Does she work at home or outside home or both?

A worthwhile discussion follows as the children try to understand Mrs. Dunderlin. They decide that she is a psychologist with office hours from 9:00 A.M. until 2:00 P.M., a sort of compromise between working inside and outside the home. I summarize our portrait of Mrs. Dunderlin and am about to move on when a hand darts directly into my face. It belongs to the red-haired little girl seated next to me, wearing a frilly, lace-trimmed dress.

Don: Oh, you wanted to say something?
Girl: Yes. And she's always cleaning!
Don: Does this fit with what we've said about her as easygoing and listening to the children?

I address this question to the entire class. Whenever there is an apparent inconsistency in the behavior of a character, I call it to the children's attention. The best discussions of character development occur at these junctures. The girl who made the observation answers immediately, even though the decision lies with the entire group.

Girl: That's true. She is easygoing. But right now she's so upset, she can't stop cleaning.

Don: Well, class, does that seem consistent? (*The class unanimously agrees.*)

Don: OK, you said there was an argument. Who spoke first?

Child: The mother did.

Don: And what did she say?

Child: "John, the children and I wish you could spend a little more time around the house."

Don: And how did Mr. Dunderlin reply to that?

Child: "If you want the things you've got, you're going to have to put up with me being on call."

Don: Does that answer ring true to you?

The children are unanimous in their agreement here. Once children get a few of the essential elements of character in place, they quickly agree on the direction of a story. The key is to help children discover what those essential elements are. Often they are connected to the wishes and desires of the main characters:

The mother wants the father home more and a more stable family.

The father wants to maintain his current situation at work and possibly with his girlfriend.

The children want a stable home life.

Don: Well, what was the outcome of this argument?

Child: It got louder and louder.

Don: And then?

Child: It got so loud that it woke the little girl up.

Don: And then?

Child: She runs into her brother's room and says, "What are we going to do? They are fighting again."

Don: And what does her brother say?

Child: The boy says, "I'm going to call my father's office tomorrow and make an appointment with him and he'd better not say 'no.'"

I decide this is a good place to end the workshop.

21

Workshop Reflection

The workshop is fast paced. The key discussion points almost always arise in relation to the wants and desires of the characters. I want children to see that plot is based on the interaction of characters, that actions have underlying motivations. The following guidelines may also be helpful in conducting this workshop:

1. *I do not write down children's suggestions.* They must listen carefully, attending to the unfolding details while maintaining a mental overview of the entire story.
2. From time to time, I stop and summarize the story thus far before going on to the next question.
3. The children are not creating this story in order to write it down. This is strictly an oral workshop.

ACTION: *Conduct a series of workshops with your students in which they begin to learn about characters and the other necessary ingredients that go into fiction.*

I suggest a series of workshops because you'll need time to get used to helping the class through the exercise. I have found this workshop to be the most effective of any I've conducted. It is also one that gets children used to the kinds of questions I'll ask in conferences about their own writing.

ACTION: *Use children's own reading books to demonstrate how writers introduce their characters.*

This ACTION can be an all-class minilesson or a small-group exercise. I often start with the entire class, then move to smaller groups with children who are struggling. This ACTION involves a range of skills, listed below in order of complexity:

- Find the main character in your book. *The main character, or the most important character, is the central person in the book. The main character can be identified as the I in the story or as the person the storyteller follows. I may ask, "How many of you have books in which the main character is telling the story is the I of the story? We call that first-person writing."*

- Find where your main character first appears. *Sometimes the author starts out with one character who gives readers the first look at the main character.*

- Notice how your author reveals the character.
  Does the character start out talking?
  Do you get to see what he looks like?
  Does someone else see him?
  Do you learn about the character through what he sees? If the book is written in the first person, you'll get a sense of what the character is like by noticing what he sees and how he reacts.
  Do you meet the main character in the midst of a thought?

- What does your main character want? How can you tell? (What's the evidence?) *This is the most sophisticated of all the questions. Writers and readers could spend a lifetime on this one. On the surface, for example, a boy might want a dog. Further reading shows that the boy spends a lot of time alone and wants companionship more than anything.*

The following examples demonstrate how three different authors introduce the main character:

Tom kept looking around when he got off the train at the depot, as if he expected Mayor Whitlock with a welcoming committee and the town band to meet him. But for my money he was lucky the mayor wasn't there with an unwelcoming committee. And, if the town band had been there, they would have been playing a funeral march and not "Hail! The Conquering Hero." (John Fitzgerald, *The Great Brain Reforms*)

In this example, Tom is the main character but the story is told from the point of view of his brother, who is the narrator. What does Tom want? Fitzgerald shows Tom looking around and introduces the possibility that people may not be so happy he is getting off the train. Is Tom looking for trouble? Why does Tom *want* trouble and why do people have negative feelings toward him?

I just got a new spider book and the first sentence is: "Spiders are the serial killers, the Jack-The-Rippers, the greatest and most famous predators of the insect world."

This may be true but it misses the point. The incredible thing about spiders isn't that they're killers. It's all the amazing ways they go about getting their food. (Ralph Fletcher, *Spider Boy*)

Here we first meet the main character in the pages of his journal. Bobby wants to set the record straight about spiders. He obviously knows something about spiders, and we can anticipate that we will probably see the world (of spiders and others) through his eyes.

Finally,

A boy in a bright blue ski jacket and Maine hunting boots stood on a snowy runway. Under rumpled black hair his crooked nose and wide brown eyes gave him an expression of good humor, although he was not amused at this moment. Yesterday he had left Boston and laid over in Anchorage in high spirits. Now he was about to run back to the friendly jet that had carried him across Alaska to this barren Arctic outpost. (Jean Craighead George, *Water Sky*)

Plot is mapped by the characters' wants. In this passage, the boy, Lincoln, seems frightened. We feel his desire to go back to where he came from. There's a difference between yesterday's elation and today's wanting to turn back. What is it? The heart says, "Move ahead," but the head says, "Wait a minute; I don't know that I like being here." Good writers grab our attention by setting up discrepancies. The main character wants one thing, but the world around him offers something else.

ACTION: *Help children to develop characters in sharing sessions or small-group workshops.*

I tell the children, "We are going to help writers to develop their characters."

Don: The way this works is the author reads the line, then we ask the author questions and the author tells us more about the character. Who will share just one line where your main character or any char-

24

acter first appears in your writing? We'll take about four questions for each author. Tim?

Tim: OK, here's one for my main character: "*He opened the door to let the dog out because the dog heard something.*"

Allison: What are their names? Do they have names yet?

Tim: Oh, I forgot. Uh, the kid's name is uh; it's Robbie.

Jan: What's his whole name? His last name?

Don: I hate to interrupt here but this is important. Tim, don't feel rushed on the name. Writers spend more time than you'd think with names. I think we'll do another workshop just on names to help. Let's have two more questions. Actually, we have two characters here, don't we, with the dog and the boy? Just concentrate on the boy for now.

Trevor: What did the dog hear?

Don: Tim has done such a good job of setting this up for us to want to know, Trevor, but right now we're just concentrating on what you'd like to know about Robbie.

Trevor: OK, what does Robbie look like?

Tim: Well, he's ten years old. He wears jeans, has brown eyes and brown hair. And he has Converse sneakers.

Don: Class, close your eyes. What can you actually see of Robbie from what Tim has said? (*The class is able to separate the age from clothes and features.*) Tim, it does help in a way to create a bit of a picture from "ten years old," and age is important in filling in a picture. We know he isn't an old man or a baby, don't we?

The children struggle to be helpful. They are just beginning to learn how to "flesh out" the barest of facts. Of course, the more information the writer can provide, the more they are able to add. Notice that I interrupted the discussion at the point of naming characters. Giving names to characters is more complicated than I used to think. I'll deal with that in the next ACTION.

Learning how to present and develop characters is hard work. But as Tim's comments about his character indicate, he is beginning to understand. In Chapter 2 I compared describing characters to cartooning: You highlight a few essential elements to convey an impression of the person. If some children need further help, try the same workshop with a group of five or six at the conference table.

ACTION: *Conduct a workshop on naming characters.*

Once children understand the idea that they have the power to name their characters, they find it easier to add other features or characteristics. When I studied children's fiction writing, I noticed that only a few children had begun to name their characters by the end of second grade. In each case, the children who used names were more advanced in their writing than the others. Later, I accidentally uncovered a developmental aspect of the problem. I was sitting on the rug in a kindergarten classroom observing children's composing with blocks when the teacher said, "All right, I want you to line up for music. I'll say your first name, then you stand up and say your last name or other name and get into line." About a third didn't know their last name, another third could remember after a delay, and another third knew immediately. I remember one boy who jumped to his feet and said, "James Michael Callahan." He knew not only his last name but his middle name as well.

I immediately went upstairs to visit the first and second grades and began to chat with the children about the nameless characters in their writing. I wanted to see if I could move some to name their characters. I came upon one second-grade boy who had written the typical good guy-bad guy story. "What's the good guy's name?" I asked.

"Good guy," he replied with a puzzled look on his face.

"Yes, I know that's the name, John, but this is one particular person. Do I have that right?"

"Yes."

"Well, if it is one person, say like you. . . . What's your full name?"

"John Fuller." (*By the end of first grade or second grade most children have acquired the full name concept. At the same time, the popular use of first names between adults, and even between children and adults, has bypassed the surname concept. Leave out the name of the family and an important part of personal development is lost.*)

"Good, let's see if we can put a full name on your 'good guy.' If he's a real person, he must have one." But John was stumped and couldn't go on. I've since learned that there are a number of reasons to explain why it was difficult for John to respond:

- Television, especially in cartoons, supplies generic characters who only occasionally have first names and rarely full names:

"earthlings," "space invaders," "creatures," "mobsters," and "policemen" abound. This is partly because the characters are so globally designed, they don't need a full name. In fact, "earth-ling" tells you all you need to know to understand the very simple plot of a Saturday morning cartoon. Children's movies and TV shows are plot driven.

- The concept "name" is closely connected to the self-concept. The more a child is aware of self, the more she is able to see others as "not self," as different.

- Awareness of the power to name develops late. This is a concept of biblical proportion. To name something, to bring a specific personality to life and give it a name and identify is quite an achievement. It is also an act of self-creation. This is why fiction is such an important genre for children.

I find it helpful to send children to telephone directories when they are choosing last names and to dictionaries for first names.

ACTION: *Select photographs from newspapers or magazines, mount them on tag paper, and use them to show children how to do quick word sketches.*

Examine the photograph in Figure 4–1. Show this photo, or one like it, on an overhead projector and ask the children to select three things about the boy's face that strike them. Cartooning requires selection. I am immediately struck by his closed eyes, his pinched mouth, and the position of his head, which is tipped slightly away from the comb. A second look has me following the eyes of the baby, which are focused on the comb, not the boy's face. She is pulling down on the comb, and most likely the boy can feel its path straight into his eye. The interaction of details like these and the tension between them creates a story.

Trust in the Family

I called our six-year-old son the day his sister was born. "Bill, you have a new baby sister. Isn't that wonderful?" I knew he was counting on a little brother. He already had three older sisters. The dead silence on his end of the line let me know just how he felt about my news.

27

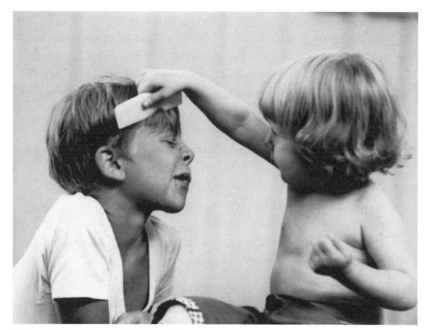

Figure 1–1. Photo of Bill and Laura

Bill was counting on a new playmate and hadn't considered any alternative. Laura, his new sister, took time from his mother. At best, he gazed at her out of the corner of his eye. They seldom interacted.

One June afternoon I was surprised to open the back door and catch a glimpse of the two of them. Bill handed a comb to Laura saying, "Fix my hair, Laura."

Laura took the comb and began to pull it through his hair. Bill wasn't sure if he'd done the right thing, but he never budged from his spot. Laura combed his hair again and again until she got tired.

Try to use photographs that show a person in a particular situation. I find that children need a lot of oral practice to become adept at noticing essential details about people.

Final Reflection

When children write fiction, they gravitate naturally toward action and plot. Our task is to lead them back to the people. It takes persistence and hard work to help them understand how to create and develop characters.

I know I am swimming against the current in these workshops on characters. Some of the difficulties are developmental and relate to children's awareness of themselves in the context of other people; some are cultural: popular media focus primarily on action. But what children achieve in these workshops builds a foundation for considering people in history, the sciences, and the arts in subsequent chapters.

Children learn from the characters they encounter in the books they read. But creating a character is far more demanding. When children write stories, they imagine characters and construct themselves as human beings at the same time.

5

Constructing Ourselves

Some years ago my wife and I gave our grandson a set of plastic hats for Christmas. The hats represented a variety of occupations: baseball player, fireman, construction worker, and pilot. When Geoffrey put on the hard hat, he played with his bulldozer in a dirt pile in his backyard, which became his own construction site. On rainy days he'd put on his pilot's hat, arrange chairs to simulate airline seats, and take off to far-away lands.

Geoffrey was in the business of constructing himself, first as a contractor and then as a pilot. As he grew older, he put aside the plastic hats and turned to Legos, and still later, to the computer. He continued to "try on" different people. When he drew a detailed color replica of an attack helicopter on the computer screen, I suspect he was also seeing what it was like to be the pilot who flew it or the engineer who designed it.

The construction of ourselves is a never-ending process. When I jotted down my list of observations about my father at age eighty-seven in Chapter 2, I couldn't help but compare my own life to his. He represents a standard by which I examine my life today. For example,

- I give money away but watch it more closely.
- As I grow older, I'm less fussy about my clothing.
- My everyday language is very similar to his: *When did you leave? What's the weather where you are? Don't be late.*
- I fear it, but at eighty-seven I'll probably have a paunch.

I see myself more clearly by considering how we are alike and how we are different. I also look back at my paragraph about the man and woman I observed in the restaurant:

Neil McGinnis leaned into conversation the way he ran his business, all chin, mouth, and chest. A pencil mustache contrasted sharply with his L. L. Bean plaid shirt. "City guy trying to look country," I figured. Fifteen strands of hair were strategically combed across his bald pate. A young woman many years his junior leaned back in her seat as McGinnis stabbed the air with a fork to accentuate his main points.

Here, I portray two characters. How does that relate to self-construction? When I imagine the life of "Neil McGinnis" at the next table, I become him. I shift my point of view, crawl inside his skin, feel myself dominating the conversation. In constructing this man I discover my own point of view: I realize that I'm not very sympathetic to him. "Likes to control everything, even lunch," I observe. Of course, I'm also wondering why the young woman is eating with him. "Ah yes, she has to dine with him; she's probably his secretary, poor soul."

When I write about the man and woman at the restaurant table, much like my grandson and his hats, I try on their personalities. I am reminded that I *have* been the pushy man. I have also been repelled by people like him. There is, in short, an element of the writer's self in every character. Writing fiction can be a process of self-discovery.

ACTION: *Look back at the characters you created in Chapter 2. Examine their traits and consider how you might shift your portrayal in a positive or a negative way.*

The art of understanding people depends on being able to put aside your own point of view completely and look at the world through their eyes. Writers strive to represent a character truthfully even if they disagree with, or even detest, that character's beliefs. Several years ago I was writing a personal memoir about the coming of World War II. In 1937–38 I knew a boy named Leo. He was my age and lived in the neighborhood. My first draft portrayed him as a boorish, sloganeering kid who wore a uniform to his Hitler Youth meetings. I began to rewrite the piece by creating a scene in which Leo romped with my dog, Rags. I showed Leo patting Rags and laughing when she licked his face. Writing about that incident also helped me to remember that his mother kissed him every morning when he left for school. Every negative character has some redeeming feature that makes him or her human.

I rewrite the scene with Neil McGinnis, inserting a small element that might give it more balance.

A young woman many years his junior leaned back in her seat as McGinnis stabbed the air with his fork to accentuate his main points. "By the way, I enjoyed the eggplant parmesan you recommended," she said, motioning her fork toward her half-eaten lunch.

This is a small touch, but at least McGinnis has to stop his lecture long enough to acknowledge her compliment. At the same time, it conveys a sense of the young woman as more than a meek audience.

In most cases, I name all my characters. In this brief vignette, the woman is unnamed. The woman's back was to me and my full attention was taken with McGinnis. Somehow I found it difficult to name a person whose face I couldn't see. Characters who have no flaws or blemishes, just like those who have only flaws or blemishes, represent one-dimensional, cardboard personalities.

Reading is also an act of self-construction. The mind takes in the author's words, imagining personalities and scenes while asking "What does this have to do with me?"

ACTION: Choose a short section of text from a book or magazine you have never read before and record what goes through your mind while you are reading it.

As an example I have thumbed through the pages of *The Human Experience: Contemporary American and Soviet Fiction and Poetry* (1989) and randomly select Boris Yekimov's short story, "A Greeting from Afar." I will put the first three paragraphs on the left column and record what I was thinking as I read the text on the right:

Bread wasn't delivered to the village everyday. So people stocked up on it: extra for themselves, and for their privately owned cattle when they were short of grain in their storage bins. On delivery days, people came early to avoid being last in line at the store and having to plead for leftovers. They sat around the entrance, the women with their knitting, dis-

A picture comes immediately. A babuska in a kind of kitchen with a place where she keeps bread, a kind of cupboard. She has a round loaf of hard bread and she is carving it. Out the window to her left is a field with cows in it and I wonder immediately, "How on earth could they ever maintain cattle with what little bread they have to eat?" My mind wanders farther. Sounds like this is just after the war was

cussing the village news and everything else.

Now they were talking about Manya Kharitonova. Her sons had come for Manya and her husband the previous autumn, and taken them to live in the central settlement of the large collective farm, which included several scattered villages.

"I look around the bus station, and there's Manya. 'Hello, how are you!' And we chatted about this and that," recounted Arkhip, a lively garrulous old man. Practically every week he was at the bus station, going off somewhere, on business or not, to Uryupinsk, sometimes even to the city, to visit relatives. "I say to her, 'I'm hurrying home to my old lady. The gardens are all in bloom now in the village. It's really beautiful!' And she, would you believe it, started to cry. 'I'll never see my village again,' she says. 'They've taken me off to some kind of barren steppe; not a garden, not a bus,' tears running right down here." Arkhip pointed with his nicotine-stained fingernail.

over, when people had so little. Soon there is old Manya and she looks like the woman in the first scene who has to share her bread with the cattle. I have a more complete picture of her now. Layers of clothing to keep her warm. They are tattered and worn, but any holes are masked by the underlayers. She is stout with a broad forehead and a mole to the left of her nose. She does not smile. Her eyes are gray, her cheeks puffy.

Arkhip wears a little black captain's hat, like those Russian peasants wear. He is fully bearded; the beard is white, accentuating his blue, dancing eyes. He is constantly smoking and puffing as he speaks. He is short and thin, smaller than Manya. But maybe I have to change my picture, because if he was off traveling, perhaps he has a slightly more businesslike look. But he is from the collective and therefore more of a farmer, a businessman farmer, and my revision may only need to give him polished boots. The two of them meet in the bus station with broad benches crowded with people dressed in peasant costume. If Manya cries, I wonder why she is there. I want to know more about her displacement, the cause of her unhappiness. Pictures, then questions. I am left with unhappy Manya, and puzzled Arkhip, the sound of quiet sobbing, her voice stammering out the reasons for her unhappiness.

33

Most of what I pictured was not in Yekimov's text. Still, the author's ability to create a scene with people waiting, knitting, and talking allowed me to visualize a group of patient peasants passing the time. I confess that I borrowed images from other Russian tales I've read. At the same time, I seized on the detail of the nicotine-stained finger to imagine Arkhip as a chain-smoking village gossip.

What does all this have to do with me? I am struck by the sadness of displacement. The government, with the help of her sons, has whisked Manya and her husband off to a more remote location on the steppes. I think ahead to the moment when old age forces my wife and me to leave our mountain home and our gardens and trails in the woodlands because we can't care for them or do the heavy work required to maintain them. As I picture Manya, I see myself. I feel her age and ponder her sense of loss. Arkhip seems a little puzzled by Manya's reaction to the good news from her old town. I wonder why he doesn't seem to understand her sadness.

Final Reflection

Reading and writing can be highly active modes of self-exploration and self-construction. When we read fiction, we encounter other selves, filtered through the author's mind and eye. The more I write fiction, the more I wonder about how other writers find inspiration for the characters in their books, what aspects of their own experience they bring to life, and what shapes they have pulled whole out of their imagination.

We have studied the people we have created as well as characters in our reading. We see plot as an extension of character and we know how to cartoon elements that reveal real personalities to ourselves. At the same time, we recognize just how personal these constructions are as we integrate them into our own lives. We now turn to an examination of character in history using the tools we've so far developed.

6

People and History

History is about people and the events that bring them together. Much of the writing in history textbooks, however, provides a panoramic view not unlike that from an airplane at 35,000 feet. The distance allows us to see a vast array of events from afar but ignores the close-up. The next two chapters will look at people in history, and the ACTIONS will help you see how to use a deeper study of people to engage yourself and your students.

For a richer understanding of events and human passion we need eyewitness accounts. We need to view historical incidents within the context of real lives and real aspirations for self, family, and country. The more we engage students in history, the more they see themselves as active participants in their own society.

Witness Ken Burns' portrayals of people in his documentary film *The Civil War* shown on PBS. Although he conveys a sense of the sweep and horror of that conflict, he never neglects the people whose lives it touches. He moves deftly between speeches, personal correspondence, period battlefield photographs, and family albums. Presidents, journalists, generals, privates, and their wives and mothers and sweethearts back home, from both the North and the South, all walk across the stage of history. War is more than the acts of military forces. Burns chose a letter written by Major Sullivan Ballou to his wife, Sarah, just before the battle of Bull Run to exemplify the pathos of war. The letter is so moving and powerful, it falls into the lines of a poem without changing a word:

> Sarah, my love for you is deathless,
> it seems to bind me with mighty cables
> that nothing but Omnipotence can break,
> and yet my love of country comes over me
> like a strong wind and bears me irresistibly

with all those chains to the battlefield.

The memory of all the blissful moments
I have enjoyed with you come crowding
over me, and I feel most deeply grateful
to God and you that I have enjoyed
them so long. And how hard it is for me
to give them up and burn to ashes
the hopes of future years when God
willing we might still have lived
and loved together and seen our boys
grown up to honorable manhood
around us . . . If I do not return,
my dear Sarah, never forget
how much I loved you, nor
that when my last breath escapes
me on the battlefield it will whisper
your name.

Forgive my many faults
and the many pains I have caused you,
how thoughtless, how foolish
I have sometimes been.
But, Oh Sarah, if the dead can come
back to earth and flit unseen
around those they love,
I shall always be with you
in the brightest day
and the darkest night
always, always, and when the soft
breeze fans your cheek,
it shall be my breath,
or the cool air your throbbing
temple, it shall be my spirit
passing by. Sarah,
do not mourn me dead. Think
I am gone and wait for me
for we shall meet again.

Major Ballou was killed in the first battle of Bull Run, just after he wrote this letter.

In such writing I meet myself and what it would mean to lose a member of my own family. In this sense, history becomes present tense. Indeed, as David McCullough has pointed out, this kind of poignant letter can be a window on the entire Civil War. The carnage was the worst in American history. Obsolete battle tactics from the war of 1812 shoved lines of soldiers against advanced weaponry. Many men died not as a result of wounds on the battlefield but because of the lack of antiseptic procedures during surgery. Some villages lost more than half the male population between the ages of eighteen and thirty-five because the young men went to war together in the same regiments. Deer Isle, the town where Major Ballou lived, was hit especially hard.

One of the best examples of history writing that focuses on people is Joy Hakim's History of the United States series. The books, written for grades 4–8, give a balanced presentation of people making real decisions. Those represented include not just leaders but people from all walks of life.

The chapter on the Second Continental Congress in *From Colonies to Country* (1993) presents the people of history through a range of approaches. A portrait of George Washington accompanies a brief statement about slavery: "There is not a man alive who wishes more sincerely than I do, to see a plan adopted for it." In another box, John Adams describes having to sleep in the same bed with Benjamin Franklin. They argue about whether the window should be open or closed.

Pictures and well-chosen descriptions introduce readers to the delegates to the Continental Congress. We begin to appreciate the breadth of personality, education, and region represented by those persons who ultimately signed the Declaration of Independence.

For some time I have struggled with curriculum matters related to social studies and the teaching of history. I have read national, state, and local curriculum guides and spoken with teachers who attempt to teach in these areas. One thing is clear: in spite of the extensive guides, teachers find it extremely difficult to be systematic in their approach to history. Social studies curricula embrace sociology, anthropology, geography, literature, the arts, and history. And while I applaud the introduction of a wide range of cultures, the emphasis on the individual and the community, and the study of local history, my objection is to the integration of these fields around behavioral objectives and goals. Teachers must understand each of the fields separately before they can integrate them effectively. In the language arts, for example, both reading and writing suffer unless the teacher understands each separately and in depth. I also believe that it is better to explore other fields through history than through a social studies approach. A systematic study of history provides a basis for understanding other fields that attempt to explain human behavior. The National Standards for History published by the National Center for History in Schools (1996) focus on chronology: "Chronological thinking," they state, "is at the heart of historical reasoning. Without a clear sense of historical time—time past, present, and future—students are bound to see events as one tangled mess" (17).

Consider also these important statements in the National Standards for History that underscore the main thesis of this book: "It is through people that children become engaged with the disciplines in the curriculum."

> To bring history alive, an important part of children's historical studies should be centered in people—the history of families and of people, ordinary and extraordinary, who have lived in children's own community, state, nation, and world.

> History becomes especially accessible and interesting to children when approached through stories, myths, legends, and biographies that capture children's imaginations and immerse them in times and cultures of the recent and long-ago past.

Much of our work in Chapters 1 to 5 can be applied to the study of historical figures, the famous and the not so famous. Historical figures also live in families and are passionately involved in their times.

The following outline lists several ways of looking at historical figures in order to understand their everyday lives and their participation in history. We begin by asking a version of the question we used in fiction:

1. What do these people want badly?
   - Personally: *status, recognition, achievement, enjoyment.*
   - Vocationally: *to be a lawyer, doctor, writer, president, a noted artist.*
2. What opposing polarities or tensions do they encounter because of what they want?
   - Within themselves: *the inner tug to go this way or that.*
   - From others: *passions and opposing forces.*
3. What do they learn?
   - Who were their mentors? Teachers?
   - What problems did they solve?
   - What failures did they encounter?
   - What did they read? write? create?
4. What personal characteristics contributed to their performance in history?
   - Did they experience personal suffering and loss?
   - What did they consciously avoid?
   - What did they most enjoy doing alone?
   - What did they enjoy doing with others?
   - Did they prefer to work alone or with others?
   - Describe the work habits of the character.
   - How did they change over time?
   - What personal or vocational issues remained forever unresolved?

ACTION: *Using the outline on page 39, consider what you can apply to an understanding of the character of Jefferson as well as the signing of the Declaration of Independence.*

There is far more in the outline than can be understood from this brief fiction recorded here. The most basic of questions, "What does Jefferson want?," ought to emerge. You may also uncover inconsistencies in wants. Indeed, this is the struggle with any person who has great ideas and aspirations.

Thomas Jefferson would be an interesting person to investigate at an important moment in U. S. history, the writing of the Declaration of Independence in 1776. Drawing on Jefferson's own writing and the writing of others, I have composed a fictional journal covering the six months prior to signing the Declaration.

Thomas Jefferson was thirty-two when he was selected to be one of Virginia's delegates to the Continental Congress in 1772. He had already established a reputation throughout the colonies for his *Summary View* and *Causes and Necessity,* a summation of grievances perpetrated by the King and parliament. It wasn't long before Jefferson was enlisted to compose three more documents: a response to Lord North's attempt to compromise with the colonies, a protest at the seizing of Ethan Allen, and the "Declaration on the Necessity of Taking Up Arms." The latter were written while battles erupted at Lexington and Concord in Massachusetts.

Jefferson had already built his magnificent home, Monticello, and passionate as he was for liberty and the colonies' cause, he was devoted to Virginia, his family, the estate, architecture, and his many individual intellectual pursuits. Honored to be selected as a delegate, he yearned to be back with his family at Monticello. In August 1775, he lost a daughter, Jane Randolph, to illness.

In the journal entries that follow, words from Jefferson's own works appear in *italic:*

January 3, 1776: Our dastardly Governor Dunmore, loyal to the crown, has seen to the bombardment of Norfolk by the British fleet. Nearly a fifth of the town blown apart and that snipe of a Governor has asked all of us to rally to the King or be called traitor.

But I am home and all is well with dear wife. Happily my fears were for naught as I had received hardly a scrip of writing from her while with the Congress in Philadelphia. I welcome the peace of home, far from the conflict of the Tidewater. I set about the business of home and stocking the land with beautiful white-tailed Virginia deer. I enjoy my roundabout walks and take stock of the simple classic lines of my dear home. I shall ride the grounds, savoring the neat lines of fences, trees, the bustle of work from servants and field workers. I catch the morning mists in the valley.

Martha is pregnant and terribly sick as before. Perhaps I can share some of her burden, comfort her in this difficult time. Duty calls me to Philadelphia but my heart and soul are here.

March 1776: I struggle to tend to flocks, the work of spring as I must return to Philadelphia. Nelson, one of the other Virginia delegates, is bringing his wife to Philadelphia and urges me to bring little Patty and Martha with me. But she would be too frail for this trip.

March 30, 1776: Notice has come that mother died at Shadwell. A sudden stroke and within an hour she was gone. There is nothing more to say.

April 20, 1776: All month maddening headaches. I can scarcely think. No relief.

May 15, 1776: I am back in Philadelphia. My head is required here. No sickness on the trip north. At least I have my violin to maintain balance to my living. Our Virginia delegation has been instructed to propose that the colonies be free and independent. We have known tyranny first-hand at Norfolk and we have much to say on this matter of separation.

June 8, 1776: Our own Henry Lee stood tall today and addressed the Congress and expressed my sentiments with melodious voice and passion. He said, "These united colonies are, and of right ought to be free and independent states." There was warm support from New England, but the Middle Colonies are indeed in the middle. Maryland, Delaware, Pennsylvania, New Jersey, and New York are not ready for the obvious. We need to separate. They call themselves friends to the measure of separation but they do not act! Obviously this is not the time to vote for independence. We postpone a decision until July 1st.

I waste my time here while the middle prances and preens. Virginia needs me for their Constitution while I rot in my seat here in Philadelphia listening to empty words and mindless pacing. In Virginia we make decisions and stick by them.

Richard Henry Lee has been called back to Virginia for family and Constitution. I am part of a committee of five instituted to prepare a Declaration. John Adams and Benjamin Franklin I know well. Livingston and Sherman, the other two members, are another matter. Sherman is treasurer at Yale and a rather stern gentleman. Livingston is my junior, bright and enthusiastic. We sit and wonder who shall write. I suggest Adams and he bluntly refuses. I ask why and he thunders like a trial lawyer in court. First, he says that I am a Virginian.

41

Second, that he is obnoxious and unpopular and no one would accept his words just because he had written them. Thirdly, he said that I could write ten times better than he. I acceded to his demand and shall write. We'll see how well my words catch their ears and hearts.

June 9, 1776: I retire to my new lodgings at Seventh and Market streets. I must escape the excessive heat of the city, have cool circulating air. I have with me a new folding writing desk I designed and had con-structed by my old landlord, Benjamin Randolph. *It claims no merit of particular beauty. It is plain, neat, convenient, and, taking no more room on the writing table than a moderate quarto volume, it yet displays itself sufficiently for any writing.* I return from my meetings at the end of each day, knowing relief from the heat of the city and the joys of solitude at my new desk for the singular work of the Declaration.

June 15, 1776: I write my draft consulting no book or pamphlet. The Declaration is familiar ground known intimately in *A Summary View*. My indictment of the King, the response to Lord North, the Virginia Constitution run hot through my veins. *I write not to find out new prin-ciples, or new arguments never before thought of, not merely to say things which had never been said before, but to place before mankind the common sense of the subject, in terms so plain and firm as to command their assent, and to justify ourselves in the independent stand we are compelled to take.*

June 27, 1776: I have completed my first draft and show it to Adams and Franklin. They suggest a few small changes which seem logical to me. Now each member of the committee has seen it and the document emerges fairly intact for the full Congress.

June 28, 1776: Hours of debate mark my document and the continu-ance of the Lee resolution postponed earlier this month for this date. There is a certain urgency to get the job done as we are desperate for alliances in the struggle.

July 4, 1776: For three solid days, July 1st, 2nd, and 3rd, the debate has raged. I sat in still agony as my words were tossed in the air like so many wood shavings. Everyone had to have their little dance with this pas-sage and that. It seemed that most knew not their politics or had any sense of language. Franklin sat at my side, his hand on my arm, as I braced for another day of the baffling onslaught. He said that long ago he had made up his mind never to prepare another paper for submission to a public body. He tried to tell me a joke about a hatter who had to change the signboard above his store due to public criticism. He kept trying to please the public and was so piqued that it eventually bore only his name and the picture of a hat.

They excised my historical arguments that there was no basis for allegiance to England. My Southern compatriots, even Northerners, couldn't accept my declaration abolishing slavery. They feared that powerful men they needed to support the document would be offended. They took out at least one-fourth of the document. But, in the end, they adopted the Declaration as amended. It is done.

ACTION: *Choose an individual central to an important decision in history or current affairs. Write one paragraph giving background, a second paragraph showing what that person wanted to achieve, and a third paragraph showing the complementary or antithetical relationship between personal desires and historical outcomes.*

It took me some time to properly research this period. I drew on three biographies of Jefferson, his letters, and the comments of others of the time. It is quite possible, however, for children to read biographies of famous and not so famous people and find enough material to write short letters or journals from the person's point of view. In a sense, they create their own artifact.

There are some excellent biographical materials written for both teachers and students. If your school can access the Internet, I suggest exploring amazon.com or the new Heinemann CD-Rom of the *Horn Book*. I'd also recommend James Percoco's *A Passion for the Past* (1998); although he is writing for high school history teachers, his lively tone sets just the right note for active student engagement with history. Students need solid materials if they are to research historical figures and bring them to life. Remember, history is more than facts. It is people with the facts.

ACTION: *Interview a historian to learn how that person approaches the subject.*

Above all, I am interested in how historians think. It is helpful to speak with someone who is an expert on the subject, and a historian who also teaches history is even better. I began by calling my local bookstore and located a gentleman who had written about the prison camp, Andersonville, during the Civil War. While he seemed like an excellent choice, I opted for someone who had actually taught history.

I interviewed Hal Bridges, a professor emeritus of history who had retired from the University of California, Riverside, over the telephone at his home in Arizona. I begin with very general questions:

Don: Tell me about your approach to history.

Hal: My approach to history is largely biographical. I try not to downplay important socioeconomic causes of historic events, but I do believe that emphasis on the personal element enlivens history. I see history as being made up to a considerable extent of the interweaving of various lives, and I think that a great deal of research exists that demonstrates the various ways that influential men and women help to shape the history of their times. Intellectual history in particular often consists of biographical sketches of influential thinkers.

Students reading a good Lincoln biography, for example, are swept along like the readers of a fascinating novel; they watch a young backwoods genius rise out of poverty and ignorance, marry and grieve over the death of children, master the law and politics, and take an eloquent controversial stand against slavery that carries him into the presidency and an agonizing successful struggle to end slavery while preserving the Union through four ghastly years of civil war. The result of such reading is in-depth understanding of the Civil War era.

Similarly, students can fight for women's rights with Susan B. Anthony, achieve heavier-than-air flight with Wilbur and Orville Wright, lead the nation through depression and the Second World War with Franklin Roosevelt, or soar into space with the astronauts.

Don: Hal, you published a biography of Daniel Harvey Hill, the Confederate general and academic. Can you tell me how you got started or give some sense of a how a historian works with that kind of research?

Hal: I must admit that when I did start on that study, I did not realize that I would have to write military history. I had trained at Columbia to write and teach social and intellectual history. I chose to study Hill first, because some of his papers were in the library of the University of Arkansas in Fayetteville, where I taught in the early 1950s, and second, because after the Civil War, Hill became an editor of a literary magazine, then a newspaper editor, and finally a college president. He seemed to fit well into my field of social-intellectual history. But when I did in-depth research in the Hill papers at West Point, the National Archives, and in various Southern history depositories, I found Hill was more than anything else a hard-fighting combat general under Robert E. Lee. His papers overflowed with fresh and exciting material on some of the great Civil War battles. Reluctantly, I turned myself into a military historian and for ten years made Hill my major research and writing project. It was a great relief when finally, in 1961, McGraw-Hill published *Lee's Maverick General: Daniel Harvey Hill.*

Don: What is your reaction to the approach that David McCullough used with his students at Cornell? He would take art pieces, photos, letters, diary entries, newspaper clippings, etc., of a particular period and then ask his students to use these artifacts as a window on their time.

Hal: I think that is a fine way to discover history.

Don: In fact, I think that was the word he used. He wanted his students to "discover" history. Another word he used was "passion." He wanted them to be passionate about history. I guess those words go together.

Hal: One small object can be a window on history. Just a narrow window, that's all you need. A whole universe opens and best of all, the student learns just how complex history can be. A person learning history in that manner isn't going to accept simplistic explanations of the present. I used to tell my master's students to choose their own topic. I'd say, "You may think you have a small topic, but if you go in deeply you'll have the pleasure of being a foremost authority on the subject." The past, of course, is infinite. There is no end to what can be discovered. I think there is a parallel in what we read about students in the physical and biological sciences. They make discoveries because they have passion and persist in what they are doing.

Don: And you certainly show that same passion about your subject. Many thanks for giving this time for the interview, Hal. I know this: I sure wish I could have been one of your students.

Final Reflection

Obviously, we cannot understand history through character alone. Nevertheless, to ignore the individual lives of the major players at important junctures in history is to lose the flavor and the personal feelings associated with the time. I recommend that for each time period, say, each ten- to twelve-year stretch, children study one person, and where possible, an ordinary citizen.

7

Opening New Doors to History

My mother read fairy tales and nursery rhymes to me when I was a child. One day, about the time I was five or so, I pointed to the books in the bookcase. I chose the thickest book behind the glass door and said, "Read to me from that one, the big one." I was curious to know what other books sounded like. I didn't know that I'd picked out a history book. When she read I knew many of the words, but when I tried to put them together they didn't make much sense. "What is this stuff?" I asked.

I remember her leaning toward me to let me know she liked the question. "History," she said, emphasizing the word with a touch of wonder in her voice, as if to imply that there are all kinds of stories in history.

"What's history?" I could tell my questions were going to go somewhere.

"It's the story of people from all over the world," she said, opening her arms as if to imply that there was lots more to say. That was the beginning of my love affair with history.

Move ahead exactly twenty years to my first year of teaching history and geography in a small New England coastal town. I did my best to inspire students with the wonder of history, with the details of events along with portrayals of major leaders as forces in national and world affairs. They filled out their worksheets, answered questions at the end of the chapters, and grudgingly wrote essays. Out of my first class of thirty-nine students, I may have reached nine, seven of whom were male. Polite students, eyelids at half-mast, waited with solemn resolution for a rescuing bell. I knew things weren't right. Enthusiasm could only take me so far. Another thirty years would pass before I began to understand why so few students enjoy history.

To get at the heart of the matter I have used a question anthropologists ask with regularity: "What's it for?" Function is closely related to meaning. Visiting a classroom, I'd point to a child's paper during writing time and ask, "What's this for?" The child often responded, "It's for the teacher." I'd ask the teacher the same question. "Oh, that's for the children so they can learn how to write." Each thought it was for the other. In the best of circumstances I'd hope that each would first see writing as a tool they could use for themselves. I'd also hope that the teacher would demonstrate her own writing for the children so that its utility might be more apparent.

If I had asked the "what's-it-for" question of those long-ago sixth- and seventh-grade history students, only a handful would have seen history and geography as something useful to themselves. What prevents children from establishing a connection to historical events? Studying history requires an understanding of many points of view and another time and place. I have to care enough about people, or be curious enough about them, to want to know what they think and why they think that way. I may care about the people I see each day, but why would I ever want to go back and understand people from another time?

Recall the story "The Boy and the Moose" in Chapter 3. You probably identified more closely with some characters in that story than with others. Perhaps you can also remember history books that offered nothing to you about your life today. For years young women only encountered men—as kings, generals, statesmen—as actors in historical events. We can't change history but we can study it whole by including the women of history.

Consider Latino, African American, or Asian children who are trying to understand a history that concerns only white males. They might ask, "What could the life of a male colonist in the eighteenth century have to do with me today?" I suspect that living in a different time, gender differences, and cultural differences distance us from people of earlier periods.

In two separate studies of gender differences in children's writing I stumbled on some facts that have relevance for teaching history (Graves 1973, 1983). The researchers found that only a few more able girls cared about current events or events back in time. A much larger number of boys cared about such events, but they focused on actions, on male leaders and wars. The girls were more interested in the characters and how they felt about events. Although these two studies examined the characters and subjects chosen by children when they wrote, they point out trends with implications for teaching history.

Too much history writing and teaching favors young men. When I was a boy, I was fascinated by battles and armies, by who won and who lost. I was attracted by the power of leadership rather than by its responsibilities. As any boy might, I dreamed of entering politics. I read a biography of Abraham Lincoln that showed him as a compassionate person who struggled through many hardships, but neglected his roles as a lawyer, husband, father, and president. I missed out on the melancholy Lincoln who agonized over tough decisions. Children need to see important figures in three dimensions.

We need to make a serious effort to search out the women of American history, beginning with Abigail Adams, the wife of John Adams. To teachers I'd recommend *A Midwife's Tale: The Life of Martha Ballard, Based on Her Diary, 1785–1812* by Laurel Thatcher Ulrich (1991), the story of a midwife in rural Maine but more particularly a carefully pieced together depiction of the everyday life of a woman in the early nineteenth century. It is in the ordinary routines of people like Martha Ballard that students will see back in time and forward to their own lives.

We need to provide many new entry points into history for our children. Using the Declaration of Independence as the medium for instruction I want to consider a variety of strategies to help children feel that history is relevant to them. The following principles should be at the heart of our instruction:

- Help children experience the many voices of history. Through role playing and informal drama, children can "try on" historical identities (include ethnicity and gender).
- Emphasize the present tense (drama does this).
- Show how a person's character shapes action in history.
- Meld history with children's voices today. Children can experiment with letters, essays, and fiction in their own writing.

There are other ways to bring history to life. Consider visiting historical sites that are in the vicinity, such as Plimouth Plantation and Sturbridge Village in Massachusetts, or the village in Williamsburg, Virginia. In these "living" museums, guides and docents wear clothes of the time and role-play the people, from craftsmen to town officials.

The following ACTIONS will allow you to make abstract historical concepts and events more immediate by using the strategies listed above. When you open the door on other periods of American history (or even other concepts in social studies), these ACTIONS will give you options to increase the entry points of history to more children.

ACTION: Experiment with drama to introduce the children to the people involved with the Declaration of Independence.

I follow the basic approaches to drama used by Dorothy Heathcote (1995) and B. J. Wagner (1998). Another useful book is Philip Taylor's *Redcoats and Patriots: Reflective Practice in Drama and Social Studies* (1998). The power of informal drama is that it creates a "history happening right now" atmosphere.

Introduce drama through role playing. To prepare the children, I read the Jefferson journal (Chapter 6) aloud as if I am Jefferson himself. I may speak with more feeling or make some asides to add more immediacy. When I play Jefferson I change my voice and become a very different person. I may put on a three-cornered hat, or fashion one from newspaper, or wear a different coat, anything to signify that I am changing identities. I want the children to be absorbed in the moment.

Jefferson: Good morning, girls and boys, my name is Thomas Jefferson. I am one of the signers of the Declaration of Independence and some say I was the main author. Actually, many people contributed to it. I'm here today to answer your questions and chat a bit about my home at Monticello, writing the Declaration, and some of my views. You can ask almost any question and I'll do the best I can to answer. When we finish I may have a few questions for you.

Child: Were you afraid of the British when you were in Philadelphia?

Jefferson: I was so intent on writing the Declaration that I suppose I wasn't. General Howe had about 30,000 troops in New York and he could have marched down and given us a good fright. If he'd captured me and the other members of the Congress, we might not be talking together today. You'd all be British subjects. How do you think you'd feel about that? You'd have a king instead of a president.

Child: I wouldn't like it. We wouldn't be free any more.

Jefferson: How about another question?

Child: What was Benjamin Franklin like? Did you know him pretty well?

Jefferson: Ah, Franklin. If it wasn't for Franklin I don't think I'd have been able to get through the writing. He had such a sense of humor. He'd say in one line what it took others to say in pages or hours of speaking. I remember his line to the Convention when people were going in all directions. "Gentlemen," he said, "We must all hang together or surely we shall all hang separately."

What do you suppose he meant by that? Does it make sense to you today?

Child: I get the second part. The British would hang them if they got caught?

Jefferson: Well done. And the first part?

Child: Maybe he meant that they were all shouting and not sticking together.

Jefferson: Got it.

There are other roles that can give children a sense of perspective on the various personalities. You might role-play Lord North, the British member of parliament who strenuously opposed attempts by the colonies to reverse their taxes. Consider Benjamin Franklin, John Adams, Abigail Adams, or a slave who heard that Jefferson was interested in abolishing slavery.

ACTION: Experiment with group role playing to help children experience history as a group.

This ACTION has five steps:
1. Preparation
2. Class preparation
3. Drama
4. Reflection and further preparation
5. Drama again

1. Preparation

Obviously, you need to prepare yourself for role playing before involving the children. I gather resources from a number of sources, including children's literature (biography, autobiography, history written for children). As I read these sources I keep a basic set of questions in mind:

- What does the person want?
- Why does the person want it or need it?
- What may the person be anxious about?
- Who opposes what this person wants?

Figure 7–1 shows how I took notes on the viewpoints of four different people. As I read I look for potential parts the children play.

I now set the stage and open the parts for each of the children to choose. We are all going to be standing on the steps of Independence Hall just at the time the final discussions are beginning on Jefferson's draft of the Declaration of Independence. We are a crowd surrounding the delegates who are about to go inside.

The following are the available parts:

Thomas Jefferson: worried and incensed by criticism
Benjamin Franklin: wise, easygoing, counsels Jefferson
John Adams: wants desperately to have Independence
Ben Franklin's son: a Tory
Deep South delegate: dislikes slave provision
New England delegate: angry at British and has suffered war, the blockade of Boston Harbor
Tory-leaning New Jersey and New York group: think Declaration a bit radical, worried about leaving mother country
John Dickinson: Pennsylvania delegate who refused to sign yet served in the army
Virginia delegates: suffered war in Norfolk, angry at British
Abigail Adams: wife of John Adams from Massachusetts
Local Philadelphia Quakers: against all arms
A slave standing with his master in the crowd
Locals: suppose all troops in New York will invade

Name	Character want?	Why want it?	Be anxious about?	Who opposes?
Thomas Jefferson	Be free of England. Write well. To be home. Free slaves.	Against kings. Be understood. Misses wife and Monticello.	Others changing his writing. Wife's health. Possible hanging.	King. Lord North. Tories. Gov. of Virginia John Dickinson.
Lord North	Tax colonies to pay for French and Indian War.	Colonies pay very low taxes compared to Britain.	Colonies breaking away. Displease king. Not enough funds for Britain.	Continental Congress.
John Dickinson	Not to break from England. Negotiate.	Work within system of mother country to be free.	Leave England too soon without country of own.	Most in Continental Congress.
Tory merchant from New York City	Stay with England. Protection from rabble rousing Patriots. Have good business.	Not be hurt by Patriots. Make a profit. Loves England, used to live there.	Not making a profit, not able to ship or import. Anger of local Patriots.	Patriots. Continental Congress. Neighbors.

Figure 7–1. Notes While Reading History

Locals: Tories, sympathetic to England, don't want to be identified
Member of the press asking questions

2. Class preparation

Children read background material about each of these roles. There is good biographical material about Jefferson, Adams, Franklin, and the Tories, and sources relating the sufferings of Virginians and Bostonians. As the children read, they can ask themselves the four questions I've listed. From their work in writing and reading they should already understand the concept, "And what does the main character want?"

You may find it helpful to have groups meet to discuss what they've learned about background and the reasons behind their point of view. They might also want to experiment by inviting children representing other points of view to their groups for discussion, for example, Southerners arguing with Boston patriots or Tories.

3. Drama

The teacher makes the transition from present to past. "We are on the steps of Independence Hall and the delegates are about to go inside. Over there is Thomas Jefferson, and there's Benjamin Franklin, etc.

"I recognize William Slade of the local Quaker meeting. Even more strange, I see Ben Franklin's son, a Tory, who isn't too pleased with what his father is doing at all."

After setting the stage and identifying who is present (some, not all) I address one of the key people, much as a member of the press might do. "Oh, Mr. Jefferson, would you please tell us what you expect to happen today? Anything controversial in your Declaration for the delegates?" I may stir the pot at this point, "And what do you think of that, Mr. Rutledge, from South Carolina?" My objective is to get the children to react to each other as if they are in role and let the play take its own natural course.

4. Reflection and further preparation

Afterwards we discuss what extra information we need in order to play our roles more effectively. I provide further readings, but it is also time for the children to write as their characters. I want them to write first person/present tense following this basic format:

- This is what I want.
- This is why I want it/need it.
- This is what concerns me, what I worry about.

The letter is the foundation of the essay. Thus, I suggest that children play their parts by writing letters to others representing similar or different points of view. For example, Franklin's son writes to another Philadelphian, a Massachusetts delegate writes to a Virginian, a worried slave owner in South Carolina writes to a delegate from North Carolina.

ACTION: *Demonstrate on the overhead how to write a letter.*

It is well known that Benjamin Franklin's son was a Tory, a real embarrassment to his father.

Dear Mr. Franklin,

I want to congratulate you for standing against your father on these important matters about independence of the Colonies. I'd always considered your father an intelligent man yet now he is moving against England, our mother country that watched over us while the French and Indians wanted to invade and make us all French citizens. I say "horrors" to that. Don't they know that what little we pay in tax will be lost in business should all this come to war? They've already put a blockade around Boston and those stubborn citizens are feeling the pinch of commerce. I know a number of those merchants who'd like to go back to the good old days of English rule.

> Sincerely,
> Nathaniel Wolfe
> Wolfe and Sons,
> Dealers in Textiles
> Port of New York

Then I take this letter and show the children how I can turn it into an essay written for the newspaper. I talk out loud as I write. "What you will see here is a shift from writing to one person to writing for the many people who will read the newspaper. I'll write now and then talk after."

Citizens of New York, it is time for serious thinking.

Have we forgotten what loyalty means? Have we forgotten that our mother country defended us against the French and the Indians? Without our staunch comrades with whom we fought shoulder to shoulder we would be forced to pay more than taxes to our masters.

Have we forgotten, dear friends, that the defense of the Hudson, the bounteous wilderness that is the source of our livelihood, costs money? I don't like taxes either but are we aware that those from England who did support us against the French are paying that bill at a rate twenty-five times higher than the taxes we call an insufferable burden?

We act in haste. If we proceed with this foolhardy act our port may be closed just as the Royal navy closed Boston. Indeed, we will remember the good days of paying the Stamp Tax. Now is the time for cool thinking.

Nathaniel Wolfe

Wolfe and Sons

I call the children's attention to some of the basic elements of essays. Essays are written for an audience of many people. They often present passionate reasoning to try to persuade readers to agree with the writer's viewpoint. I come back to the central question in Chapter 1, "What does the writer or reader want?" People write essays because they want other people to think and feel a certain way or do certain things. A child reads an essay and I ask, "What does this writer want you to think and feel or do?" The child writes an essay and I ask the same question.

Nathaniel Wolfe, in the essay above, wants the other colonists not to break away from England. To be persuasive, he presents evidence:

1. The British provided loyal defense during the French and Indian War.
2. The defense costs money.
3. The people in England are paying more than the colonists.
4. The New York port may be closed and many will lose their livelihoods.

5. Drama again

In the next scene, the delegates are just leaving Independence Hall, having agreed to the provisions in the Declaration. Several members of the press ask them questions. I want people to react from their own point of view as the same characters. Because of their earlier preparation, children usually have no difficulty responding. Some children may wish to write plays dramatizing various points of view or articles for a newspaper composed before and after the Declaration is completed.

ACTION: Interview a local historian or someone who has lived through or knows about a particular event you may be studying.

In Chapter 6, Hal Bridges suggests that local history can be a valid way to involve children in the study of history. I suggest that children have practice in interviewing before anyone visits the class. You may find "The Lively Art of the Interview" (Graves 1989) helpful.

Final Reflection

This chapter attempts to show ways to introduce historical concepts to a broad spectrum of children. History unfolds through the interaction of many points of view. Focusing on people makes history more immediate to children, who are too often served only a bland diet of worksheets and end-of-chapter questions.

Children need many different entry points into history. Role playing and informal drama are one way they can try on the personalities of real figures in history and begin to understand other points of view. A key developmental issue for children is learning that others can have different desires and intentions, that there are different ways of thinking.

Role playing and drama also help children experience the concept of voice, which can greatly assist their writing. Strategic encounters with letters, essays, and poetry in preparing for drama allow children to practice seeing from various perspectives. Once again, history is best understood through people rather than through abstract texts.

8

Artful Thinking

I've often thought that painters, composers, writers, and scientists have much in common. They feast on details. They are in a constant state of composition, working at something that consumes them. When an idea forms "in their heads," they can't wait to get to the canvas, the computer, or the piano.

We need to know more about how artists think, how they discern commonality of experience. The artist moves to a different pace, one that is much needed in today's schools. Life speeds up, and we lose our direction in our rush to prepare children for "the" good life. Unfortunately, we forget that the arts are what makes life worthwhile. The artist slows the world down, simplifies it with exquisite choices, then brings us to meet a different side of ourselves in an object, melody, or line. Elegant thinking that is reflective of a different engagement with the universe is indeed the superior thinking that is often bypassed in our schools.

We need to experience artistic thinking in order to encourage artistic thinking in our children. I want to look closely at one artist, Georgia O'Keeffe, a woman ahead of her time in her art and her thinking. I will draw on *Portrait of an Artist* (Lisle 1986) and *Georgia O'Keeffe: American and Modern* (Eldredge 1993). In one sense this chapter will allow us to observe her thinking about the visual world and try to apply some of it ourselves.

Born in 1887, Georgia O'Keeffe grew up on a Wisconsin farm and showed an early interest in art, especially painting. From the beginning she was captivated by natural forms. O'Keeffe studied at the Chicago Art Museum, at Teachers College, Columbia, in New York City, and at the University of Virginia at Charlottesville.

Early in her career she taught art at a women's boarding school in Virginia and in 1911 was offered her first full-time position as a public school supervisor in Amarillo, Texas, where she was responsible for art and penmanship. One of her indirect mentors, Arthur Wesley Dow, the head of the fine arts department at Teachers College, Columbia, had praised the freshness and freedom of children's ideas. Unfortunately, the state mandated the use of copybooks as the approach to teaching art. Children were expected to copy exotic forms from drawing books. O'Keeffe fiercely opposed their use and told the children not to buy them. The Superintendent insisted that she obey state law and a struggle followed between O'Keeffe, the administration, and the state. At the end of the school year the books had not been bought. But it was through her teaching in Texas that she fell in love with the wild beauty of the West.

Later, after a brief period of working in New York City, she returned to Texas to teach at Texas State Normal School, where she was able to exercise more freedom in her teaching. She was a forceful, inspiring teacher who encouraged her students to take risks and to discover the world in which they lived. In Texas, as elsewhere, she was aloof in her dress and manner. She cared little for social convention, took long walks alone on the range, wore flat shoes and long skirts, and attended few teas put on by the women of the town. One woman who asked why she wore her hair so simply got a quick O'Keeffe retort, "Because I feel like it!"

She first achieved recognition in 1916 through a showing of her work by Alfred Stieglitz, whom she eventually married. Stieglitz not only gave her her first show, he remained her most important critic until his death. Stieglitz was an internationally known photographer who also pioneered the introduction of more avant-garde art into the United States through his own gallery. When he saw Georgia O'Keeffe sketches he exclaimed, "At last we have an original American artist not influenced by the Europeans."

Wherever she resided she was influenced by nature whether in New York City, Lake George in upper New York State, or New Mexico. She is known for her large flower studies, especially the black iris, and the skulls she painted in the desert of New Mexico and the Southwest.

She was very conscious of being a woman artist among men. A frank, sometimes contentious woman, she usually spoke her mind, defying public convention. She consistently sought simplicity, and in

her home preferred plain walls, basic wooden furniture, and little dec-
oration. Her canvases usually focus on the exceptional beauty of a
chosen object. O'Keeffe spent her last years in New Mexico and died
in 1986 at the age of ninety-nine.

As you read the following selections, consider what this artist wants
and how she relates to the world. I have taken direct quotes from
O'Keeffe's work (via the Lisle biography), classified them, and then
brought them together in brief statements, letters, or essays. Her
actual words are in italic. At the end of each selection an ACTION
will help you to consider artistic thinking in your own life.

A Way of Seeing

Georgia O'Keeffe spent her early years teaching in public school and
university. She was teaching in Texas when her first sketches caused a
stir in New York art circles. O'Keeffe's words

> When I teach my main point is not to teach them to paint pictures but
> to show them a way of seeing. When I teach art I teach it as the thing
> everyone has to use. There is art in the line of a jacket and in the shape
> of the collar as well as in the way one addresses a letter, combs one's
> hair or puts a window in a house.

led me to write the following fictional letter to Alfred Stieglitz, which
is intended to show her views of teaching in Texas and to apply her
teaching ideas to schools.

> Dear Alfred,
>
> I know you wish me to come to New York to paint full time. And I
> would like nothing better. You forget, however, that I owe much to my
> students. *When I teach my main point is not to teach them to paint pictures*
> *but to show them a way of seeing. When I teach art I teach it as the thing*
> *everyone has to use. There is art in the line of a jacket and in the shape of*
> *the collar as well as in the way one addresses a letter, combs one's hair or*
> *puts a window in a house.* Know with conviction what simply looks
> good to you.
>
> I submit that if I give fresh eyes to my students, then I give still

fresher eyes to myself. Imagine it, 31 sets of eyes all discovering anew. Can there be anything more invigorating?

Sincerely,
Georgia O'Keeffe

The next reflection is based on her dealings with the Texas State Legislature's decision that children should copy figures from books.

If schools would listen to me, and there's no assurance they will, I'd say, "stop trying to make all the children like everyone else." Have you forgotten that no one sees the same sunset or flower with the same eyes, or the same frog? Have you considered what will happen if you succeed? Every child will think she sees nothing unusual. Very soon she will become bored with the world.

ACTION: *First, choose a room or some location familiar to you. Next, choose ten objects there that are pleasing to you, that you consider beautiful. Finally, write about why you consider three of these objects beautiful.*

This ACTION borrows from my fictional letter from O'Keeffe to Stieglitz, to see with our own eyes that which is art, what we consider to be beautiful. Right now I'm toying between choosing between two locations in my home—my study and the living room.

I have made a list of ten objects from the living room. As O'Keeffe has recommended, I am looking for art "wherever it may be found." And although it may be impossible to ignore, I'm trying hard not to let the history of any object influence me. Some items have sentimental value, but I deliberately want to see objects as if for the first time. The ten are:

1. Bench: a simple, nine-foot church pew with curled walnut ends and a one-inch walnut back.
2. Stained-glass frame: a twelve-inch-square frame of a madonna and child in purple, white, and red stained glass.
3. Wooden statue: a small mahogany sculpture of an African woman, arms folded in front of her.
4. Wrought-iron silhouettes: little girl feeding three cats.
5. Grandmother clock: seven-foot, glass-sided, Howard Miller grandmother floor clock, oak frame, white and gold clock face.

6. Stone vase: solid stone, except for a drilled opening in the top for flowers, gray and white, slightly concave sides.
7. Antique rocking chair: caned back and seat, curved armrests, bird's-eye maple facing at top of chair back.
8. Dark green bottle: fifteen inches tall, five inches wide at the base, tapering up to a narrow neck with a quarter inch rim at the top.
9. Pair of antique sperm-whale teeth: eight-inch-long polished ivory teeth with scrimshaw of an Indian on each.
10. End table: twenty-four-inch oak table with shelf below, legs curving up to support an eighteen-by-twelve-inch top with four dowels on either end, giving a lyrelike look. Dark mahogany stain.

As I make the ten selections I am trying hard to understand what I consider beautiful and what common aesthetic attributes these objects represent to me. I quickly notice that the curve is very attractive to me. Different textures, especially as they contrast to what is near them, is another. The three I have chosen to describe more fully are the bench, the stone vase, and the small mahogany statue of an African woman. I recognize, as O'Keeffe observes, that each of these pieces is beyond words.

Visual art tries to do what words can't. It leads the viewer to feel and think and even act in a new way. My task in describing these three objects is to take words as far as I can to show what I consider beautiful rather than to say "this is beautiful" or "this is elegant."

Church pew

As I write, I face the pew at the other end of the living room, about fifteen feet away. Four large four-by-six-foot picture windows behind the pew invite a view of two mountains as well as the treetops on the tree line lower down the hill. We installed these windows because we wanted to bring the feeling of the outdoors inside. The simple lines of the wooden pew complement the view. The base, the seat, and the back of the seat are parallel to the floor. Except for the walnut back and the walnut armrests, the bench is painted white. The curved armrests seem a trifle elegant, but their polished wood invites the hand to touch. The whole suggests, "This is all you need to be alone with God." The pew invites the viewer to rest, to bide a while with a God who cares.

African statue

I had taken little notice of this sculpture until the ACTION on beautiful things. Carved of smooth, well-polished mahogany, the woman stands demurely with her right hand crossed over her left at the waistline. Her hair is parted in the middle over a broad forehead. I notice the downcast eyes, the pursed lips, full bosom, and folded hands, and sense a dignified but subservient presence. I am uneasy that this woman feels she must bow her head before me. She is too strong for that.

Not unlike the church pew the statue has simple lines and features. I realize that I am attracted by simplicity, restraint, and dignity.

Stone vase

The vase, like the bench and African statue, invite me to touch, as if something will be lost unless I trace the outlines with my fingers. I wonder if I am drawn to smooth textures or to simple curves. The stone vase is curved on the left side, but on the right it is one long, uninterrupted curve carrying the eye from the neck to the base. The artist has taken a simple, natural stone that would normally be found outside, in a garden or woodland (especially in New Hampshire or Maine) and invited it indoors. The gray-white textured granite is heavy. On one side, a slight concavity invites touch and adds an air of lightness to an otherwise heavy object. For me beauty seems to involve the twin notions of polarities and ambiguity: the stone vase belongs outdoors but is indoors, is hard and heavy but invites touch, and will hold delicate flowers. A question arises: "Why is something so heavy needed to hold something so light?" Unanswered questions allow for continuous participation in the beautiful. The artist struggles at the edges of thought and the viewer perceives more clearly what is involved in being human.

Consider the following short piece I have written based on Georgia O'Keeffe's ideas before you try the ACTION that follows. Again, O'Keeffe's words are in italic.

> *Learn what you like of nature in all its exquisite forms.* If you have been attracted by the graceful curve of a tulip leaf or have let its flower drop, petal by petal, until only the stem remains, know that you enjoy this. *Your eye has discovered its own kind of beauty and one week ago you were taken in by the poignant day by day course of events that left a gentle pile of tulip petals on the dresser top.*

If you love something you will be affected by it. When I am affected by an object, it no longer resembles the original object. *In this sense there is nothing less real than realism. The details are confusing. It is only by selecting, by eliminating, that we get at the real meaning of things.* So as I paint I say "This can go and that can go." Most people think that exaggeration involves expanding something. I say there is truth to that. But, twist it another way and I say that moving to simplicity is its own kind of exaggeration. Either way, we exaggerate to get at the truth of the matter.

ACTION: *Choose an object that is pleasing to you. Draw it once to see it anew. Take a clean piece of paper and draw it a second time, as if you had never seen it before. Draw the object a third time from memory.*

I wrote this ACTION three days ago. It took me that long to summon up enough courage to try it. In the past, I've invited readers to try what I have already done. But here, the playing field is level. We start at the same place. I wonder if I can overcome my sense of ineptness. Figure 8–1 shows my three trial pencil sketches of a pottery pitcher. You may wish to use watercolor, oils, or charcoal as you experiment with this ACTION.

As I sketch I think of what Karen Ernst (1994) says in *Picturing Learning*:

> As I look at a person or object I pretend that my pen is touching it, and I begin to follow the line of the subject, letting my pen move along the edge. . . . When I draw I try not to look at my paper. I use the drawing to help me notice first, then look closer, to move inside where my experience is.

Trial 1   Trial 2   Sketch from Memory

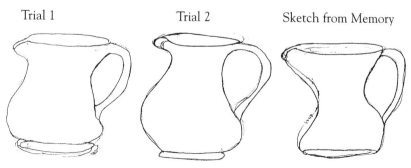

Figure 8–1. Three sketch trials

What have I learned from trying this ACTION?

- More than ever, I appreciate the lovely curved lines of the pitcher.
- A flowing line is not easily replicated.
- Successive sketches, like successive drafts in writing, help me to see more and appreciate more.
- If I were to try it again, I would sketch more quickly.
- I would study the proportionate relationships of the objects to learn what to look for before sketching.
- I lack the skill to render my emotional response to the object.
- I am struck by the similarity between drawing and writing: practice helps.

I am struck by how much more the pitcher affects me when my hand and eyes try to take in its simple curved lines. I don't think I will ever look at pitchers in the same way again. The colors add a great deal to the effect the pitcher has on me: two yellow lemons on indigo blue with a glimpse of white on the inside. The pitcher's colors reflect the bright abundance of lemons on the Amalfi coast of Italy, where I acquired it. I think I was affected by its lines but didn't realize how much until I tried to sketch it.

Delight in Simplicity

I dislike clutter. I like the smooth, simple lines of a clean desk, with all papers tucked into their correct files. But as hard as I work on correspondence, on reshelving books, on slotting CDs back on the rack, clutter abounds. I wince when I open the door to the attic, a graveyard of old computers, copiers, FAX machines, and boxes of photos.

The cluttered aspects of my life are too often a measure of my susceptibility to the marketing net cast by vendors of electronic equipment. But the more cluttered my life becomes, the fewer important decisions I make, the less time there is for living. The material life requires speed, maintenance, lists, and appointment books. Busyness urges me to hurry past the simple curves and joyful colors of the pitcher, the serene lines of the church bench, my wife at the breakfast table.

I return to Georgia O'Keeffe, who worked her entire life to redefine simplicity. She bought a home in New Mexico because of the invitation of a door opening in an adobe wall. She lived in the Southwest, because as she said, "Half my work was already done for me in the simplicity and grandeur of the lines of mountains, desert, and sky." O'Keeffe dressed in black and tied her hair back, yet she focused on the vibrancy and surprise of color.

O'Keeffe's search suggests a simple question: "How can schools invite children into artful, meaningful living focused on real thinking?" Years ago I invited a British Infant School director to visit one of the classrooms in a school building where I was an administrator. His comment as he left one of the first-grade classrooms has lived with me to this day: "Got quite a supermarket in there, haven't you, Don?" Suddenly, I saw the room in a new light. Its organization showed little focus or aesthetic awareness. There was an abundance of stimulation (of which I was justly proud), but no evidence of selection. A room offering variety within aesthetic simplicity leads to the best kind of reflection; and reflection is at the heart of the educated person, the contemplative scientist, the wise historian, and the mathematician.

Georgia O'Keeffe's advice is "Paint what you love." Choose something that fascinates you and reach into the heart of it. Of course, the contradiction is that the more you reveal, the more mystery remains.

ACTION: *Choose an object that interests you. Continue to sketch it until your study of line and texture reveal something new to you.*

I begin by choosing something I like, as O'Keeffe suggests. I will know that I am generally affected by the object but I'm hoping that in sketching something will be revealed to me. With good fortune perhaps I can show what is beyond words. Unfortunately, words are much more my currency and I suspect the opposite will be the case. Nevertheless, I must begin to learn with a pencil in my hand.

I spent about half an hour looking for the right object. I finally chose a crystal wineglass, placed it on a shelf at eye level, and began to sketch (see Figure 8–2).

How frustrating and exhilarating! My unskilled hand couldn't respond while my judgmental eye watched the entire operation. I found it useful to pick up the glass and feel the heft of it, trace the markings cut along the sides, and run my fingers down the stem and over the base. I followed the Russian psychologist Vygotsky's (1962) advice in *Thought and Language*, "When trying something new increase the sensory aspects of learning." My hand helped my eye to discover the glass for the first time.

I made six sketches, one of which I quickly abandoned. I learned that it was better to start again than to try to "fix" a drawing. I can't

Figure 8–2. Five wine goblets

tell if the sketches show improvement, but I know I continued to discover what was beautiful about the wineglass. It invites the lips to the rim. The long stem flows up to the cup, suggesting elegance. Another time I would pour red wine into the cup and work from there. As with the Italian pitcher, I will now observe all wineglasses in a different light. I will be asking, "And how is this wineglass beautiful?"

Two days later I look at my five trial sketches of the wineglass. I worked very hard to be accurate, first concentrating on the bowl in the second, then shifting to shading and a longer stem in the third, and a more impressionistic rendering in the fourth and fifth. I find myself most taken by my impression of the glass and the lines of the bowl in the second as well as by its overall simplicity.

Greater Truths in Small Objects

In each of the ACTIONS in this chapter we have been reaching into the unknown, trying to discover the beautiful. Georgia O'Keeffe has been our guide. I pick up my pencil and begin to feel the beginning of answers to the deeper questions all artists ask.

Consider the words of Georgia O'Keeffe (Lisle 1986, italicized) and my reflection on them.

When I work I want to reach toward the unknown. There are no charts to map my way. *It is the wilderness I enter. I know there is something to be discovered, something to be crystallized perhaps.* For instance, there is a truth to be discovered in the ruffled rose.

Of course, sometimes I reach and it all turns stale. I have to start over again as I try to grasp truth in the dark.

I wanted to paint bones from the desert because of their beautiful shapes. When I paint they are not bones to me. In fact, the bones are the equivalent of the desert. Those bones cut sharply to the center of something that is keenly alive there. There is a solitude and a kind of untouchableness there. The bones know no kindness in their beauty. I reached for bones and found a truth in their beauty.

ACTION: *To Georgia O'Keeffe bones represented the desert. Look for an object that captures the essence of a place. Begin to sketch it and evalu-*

ate it: "yes, good choice," or "no, bad choice." In this ACTION you are reaching to explore this object in relation to a broader context.

I headed outside with my clipboard and pencil searching for something that might exemplify the New Hampshire outdoors. I chose two granite boulders, one of which was suspended on top of the other. I had a hard time capturing the weight of the top one. I didn't have the technical skill to pull it off. In New Hampshire, there is a solid, stolid weight to the landscape and the broken pieces of granite scattered everywhere. I liked the notion of choosing granite, but I had left out one important aspect, selecting what to me was beautiful. This ACTION is simply going to take more time. I'll need to go outside and look again.

I feel better about this sketch (see Figure 8–3) but what still bothers me is that I haven't rendered the *effect* of the rock on me. I like its lines more than those of my first choice. What is it about the rock that elicits my strong response?

Figure 8–3. Second try

Criticism

We encounter critics everywhere. I find my toughest critic within myself, yet it is humbling to expose oneself to the judgment of others.

When I taught a writing course at the university I had a universal rule: "No apologies!" In fact, I had an apology piggy bank in which students put fifty cents every time they apologized. We used the money to hold a party at the end of the course. I asked only that students make their best effort. Making mistakes, even failing, is an essential part of learning. False apologies to attract compensatory praise can become a temporary haven but they stand in the way of experience.

How hard it is to find a good critic. I want honesty, but I also want encouragement and guidance to help me to write, sketch, paint, create to the best of my ability.

ACTION: *Who do you go when you have finished creating something? Write for five minutes about why you choose that person. Or, write a short letter telling them why you go to them.* Here is what I imagine Georgia O'Keeffe might say:

Dear Lily,

I know I'm quite direct and would like to be my own critic. After all, if I can't tell what pleases me, how can I pass this important job on to someone else? Still, having said all this I need a person in whose taste I have confidence. *Then, and this may surprise you, when I paint and I think I might be just a little bit good, I'd rush to that person and show it to them. Stieglitz was that person for me.*

We all need critics in whose taste we trust. Lily, go find that person and you will know he or she is good for you because the next day you will paint with new eyes. You will say, "Yes, this is uniquely me." Remember, you only need *one* good critic, not a board of governors.

With affection,
Georgia

I know where I go with my writing. My wife, Betty, is my first and most important critic. She knows my style, my ideas, and she is a no-nonsense critic. Donald Murray has been a fine critic, and my editor, Lois

Bridges, asks good questions from a reader's point of view ("Don, don't you need to say more about this?" or "I think you've lost your readers here"). I don't write for a committee, and I have enough experience by now to know what helps me as a writer.

But I am just beginning to draw, and I have no idea how to select someone who will help me. I fall back on what I know about writing. Here is some of the advice good critics have given me:

- This is what I see you doing. I think this is what you are trying to do. Did I get that right?
- This is what I find interesting here.
- This is what is working for me.
- This is what you need to consider next.
- Watch while I show you some things that will work.

ACTION: *Interview a working artist to begin to appreciate how artists view the artistic process and the place of art in their own lives.*

To bring life into learning we need to talk to working artists. We will be doing more of this in Chapter 10.

Juliette Hamelecourt is known internationally for her work in embroidery and watercolors. At eighty-six, she remains alert and is still painting, exhibiting, and selling her watercolors.

I prepared a few questions in advance of our interview:

1. Why is art important to you?
2. Tell me about what you are working on right now.
3. I am concerned about art in the lives of children. What can we do to bring art into our classrooms?

I also had in mind Georgia O'Keeffe's words about teaching art as a way of seeing.

I interviewed Juliette Hamelecourt by telephone at her home in Cleveland Heights, Ohio.

Don: Why is art important to you?
Juliette: I cannot separate it from my life.
Don: Well then tell me about art and your life.
Juliette: I grew up in an atmosphere of art. My grandfather was a musi-

cian and a good one. I was not gifted for music. I was visual. Everything made an impression on me. That is a gift too if one learns to internalize it. As children in our grandparent's vacation home we were read to, taken to concerts and museums. We were also made to perform, to recite. Earlier than that when I was five years old, I experienced my first great visual delight. My father had been drafted during the first World War to create munitions factories in England to help defend the Allies. On Sunday mornings he allowed me to walk with him through the great machinery halls. The way the machinery turned and hummed was an awesome spectacle. Since bombs are pointed there were heaps of steel shavings. There was oil on them, which gave them, like oil on a rain puddle, the most beautiful colors. Just a heap of discarded things but an epiphany.

Don: How do you react to this statement by Georgia O'Keeffe? "When I teach my main point is not to teach them (my students) to paint pictures but to show them a way of seeing. When I teach art I teach it as the thing everyone has to use. There is art in the line of a jacket and in the shape of a collar as well as in the way one addresses a letter, combs one's hair or puts a window in a house." Know with conviction what looks good to you.

Juliette: I agree to O'Keeffe. When I was in Houston last month I visited the garden of Jeanne and Mickey Klein, collectors of contemporary art. I saw a fabulous sculpture made of a real man's cotton shirt, which had been coated with a metallic substance. It was caught in the action of falling, crumpling, with the sleeves hanging, a sort of pyramid that was both imaginative and beautiful. We must never be taught that art has to be pretty.

Don: What do you do that has you associated with art?

Juliette: In life, before World War II, I had the means to be a collector, even at a very young age. In doing so I helped emerging artists with their first major exhibition. In Belgium in the late thirties there was a lot of foreboding because of the Spanish Civil War. The art echoed or even prefigured the horrors to come. I had worked with the Society of Friends in finding temporary homes for Spanish children separated from their families or left to roam on battlefields. Newsreels of the period influenced me very much. I lived in a sedately beautiful home in Brussels. It was very Louis XV in style and tone but I felt like shaking up the complacency in the neighborhood. I built a house completely out of style, a red brick, squat, with large windows and lots of whiteness and light on the inside and brought back from Spain monastery doors that had actual bullet hole marks and a dark oaken stairway that also had been mishandled. The effect was very strong, matching my art collection of Boonens, de Bruyckers, Permeke, and Otto Dix among the German artists. Indeed, I had, not necessarily on the walls but in portfolios, things like the illustrations from the book *All Quiet on the Western Front* by Erich Maria Remarque. I was also attracted by the surrealist painters, many of whom I came to know very well: Magritte, Delvaux, Breton, Man Ray, Varo. I was there when Meeseng opened the first surrealist exhibition in his London gallery. To me Surrealism drowned the despair of not being able to do better than the great masters of other periods. Sort of "since we cannot as individuals change the world, we'd better make a tongue-in-cheek kind of spoof about it all." I was in Belgium when the Nazis invaded. In 1941 I ended up in the United States.

Don: Did your art collecting continue?

Juliette: No, I had no money. I worked part-time for a Free French newspaper. I did the women's page. We had a small budget. I was also assigned the "Lonely Hearts" column, a culinary column, and by and by some movie reviews and art critiques about French artists in the U. S. This furthered my knowledge of art; it made it current. I was passionately in love with art and never missed a show. However, the idea of painting like I do now intimidated me. I had no confidence in myself.

I watched my painter friends. When I was seven my father, who was an amateur watercolorist himself, let me have lessons from a Chinese Buddhist monk, who taught me to grind my own pigments and to follow the strict precepts of the Tao of painting. He used to yell at me for not meditating until a picture was set in my mind and that I only had to put it down on paper. The technique is still with me. You don't forget how to ride a bicycle. All you need is a little practice. So when I was fifty-eight and a World Craft Council representative in Haiti, I designed tapestries for which I have become known. I just concentrated and then with an indelible Magic Marker I drew on handwoven cotton the things my students and I were to embroider in brightly colored threads. That was for myself very late in life. That's because I had no confidence in myself. I had one lesson in Cleveland. There was an advertisement for an art class for senior citizens. That was the only class I ever took. The one thing that remains with me is my sense of humor that I got from the Surrealists.

When I paint it's a story. Everything is a story. Why create something that has no journey into your deepest self? You begin the telling of the story. It's like a circle. The story develops and it concludes when it comes back to you. It starts with a full image and then it takes on a life of its own and then it comes back to my innermost feelings. That happens with almost everything I do. It becomes my treasure chest.

Don: I find the same thing happens in writing. I have an inkling of an idea. It's an indistinct image or idea and I have to follow it to understanding. In that sense it comes back to me and becomes part of me. I am not the same person as before. The sculptor Henry Moore said something, that what we try needs to be near impossible and that is how we gain depth in our deepest self. Do I have the gist of what you were talking about?

Juliette: Yes, I think so.

Don: I suspect you have some ideas about children becoming involved with art.

Juliette: Indeed I do. I was five when that monk exposed me to absolute art. He didn't expose me to pretty flowers. I had to really work for that image in my skull. I don't think children need to be taught. For example, children don't need to be taught that "see, the shadow belongs over there." They need to be exposed to as much art as possible. On the other hand, they do need to be taught the way to work with the tools and how to use the materials. The teacher should be acquainted with, say, the work of Ralph Meyer: *The Artist's Handbook of Materials and Techniques*. The teacher should teach the right way to use diverse materials even at a very tender age. This enhances creativity.

The child should be let alone. It must come from within the child. Never say to the child what subject to consider or what colors to use. I like to work with Chinese brushes.

Don: That was a gift wasn't it, to be exposed to the Buddhist monk?

Juliette: An enormous gift. Children have an openness to art that is unparalleled. They have to be allowed to be free. If that happens they will turn out good art if they are encouraged to make the effort required. Art is not a game.

Don: I want to thank you for this interview. I look forward to the day when we will meet face to face.

I was struck by a number of things in talking to Juliette Hamelecourt. First, I had not thought about the importance of the grotesque (as in the bullet holes in her doors in Brussels) as an important facet of art. Beauty is important, but the grotesque can also express what the artist wants to say. Second, I was struck by her emphasis on having no topic or forced subject choice for children. Finally, her circular notion of the composing process is elegant. That is precisely what happens in writing. We begin with an idea, go on a journey that has storylike qualities, and ultimately come back to the idea that started us on our way.

Final Reflection

We have followed Georgia O'Keeffe, as a guide to viewing the world and the world of art.

Learning to see is as basic to visual art as to verbal art. We push words to say something. Some artists choose clay, paint, music, or textiles. The collective effect, the emotional impact is enough for the artist. By sketching, I discover the object as well as the truth about the object. The hand helps the eye to know a different universe.

We have to silence the punishing critic who holds back the performer in all of us. For the teacher-artist, art is never wrong, it is simply unfinished.

9

Let the Arts Lead

The arts are one of the most fragile areas in the American education curriculum. They are easily excised when budgets are cut, ignored in assessments, and scheduled out of any school day to make way for early dismissal or special programs. We have little tradition of valuing the arts in America. Artists, according to the conventional wisdom, are a frivolous lot, who do nothing for the economy and seem more bent on playing than on looking life dead in the eye.

In mainstream America, the philosophy is something like "get a good job, have a family, acquire nice things, take vacations, and make sure the kids get a good education." We are very conscious of living in a global economy and we have a gnawing fear that suddenly our job will be outdated, noncompetitive, irrelevant.

The evening news reflects a shift in our national anxieties. During the Cold War, reporting centered on our worries about the Russians and nuclear annihilation. Now a stream of economists and Wall Street experts produce economic forecasts regarding our investments and everything that might affect our finances. Unfortunately, we too have become "commodified." We need *things* to measure our success, to show that we are successful. We have computers, cellular phones, digital cameras, houses with vast carpetlike lawns, acreage, vacations in Hawaii, boats, and vans. We work at high speed, reorganizing our time for even greater efficiency, and exercise furiously.

We lean into our computer screens and live alternately between the shadows of the superbowl on TV and the incoming e-mail or text on the screen. Waste from these giant production engines litters the landscape. Drug abuse, anxiety, sleeplessness, severe depression, and alcoholism blight our lives. Our recreation craves extremes: rafting, motorboat racing, jet skis, downhill racing on the double black diamond, bungee jumping, or parachuting. We relive the *Titanic* disaster, follow the Oklahoma City bombing, or stay glued to the coverage of the O. J. Simpson trial and the travails of the president. Slow the pace and we sit like lumps on the couch. More and more people resemble machines. Life spins us in a whirlwind of getting and wasting and boredom.

Curriculum, Learning, and the Arts

The arts must play a greater role in curriculum. First, they allow us to step back and see more clearly the world around us. Marshall McLuhan called the arts the "antenna of a civilization." We need better antennas on both the personal and cultural levels. Second, the arts provide a rare kind of elegant thinking sometimes considered superior to "word thinking." Art brings together in one place an image and a response that goes directly to the heart of real thought. (Advertisers have long known that an image can cause a person to act long before words have an effect.) Third, the arts are an end in themselves. They are what makes life worth living.

We are familiar with the work of scientists checking ozone layers over Antarctica, take borings in the ice cap to explain geologic history, testing air and water for purity, and investigating why frogs have deformed appendages. These are the litmus tests for our biosphere, the early warning of approaching disaster. The arts explain who we are to ourselves. The sculptor and the painter reach beyond words to express truth, the truth of human life.

Beyond Words

Goethe, the noted German writer and philosopher said, "We ought to talk less and draw more. I, personally, should like to renounce speech altogether and, like organic nature, communicate everything in sketches" (Hjerter 1986, 16). I was surprised to find how many professional writers see the nonverbal arts as superior to their own craft with words. "If any man has any poetry in him he should paint it, for it has all been said and written, and they have hardly begun to paint it. Every man who has that gift should paint," says Dante Gabriel Rosetti, a nineteenth-century British poet (48).

Vera John-Steiner (1986), one of the translators of Vygotsky, considers different patterns of inner speech in her research about the nature of human thinking. Many of our great thinkers project a flow of images.

> Evidence of a lifelong pattern of using visual and kinesthetic pictures was found among Einstein's papers at Princeton; among these was a description of a "thought experiment" he conducted at age sixteen. After Einstein read Maxwell's theorem which proposed to explain light waves, he "imagined himself riding through space, so to speak, astride a light wave and looking back at the wave next to him." (85)

John-Steiner also observes that physicists and biologists prefer visual modes of thought, while social scientists use inner speech (with words) as their dominant mode of cognitive representation. Koestler, a novelist, and Arieti and Schactel, who write about creativity, point out that a reliance on verbal concepts alone "may lead the scientist to a certain rigidity of thought which can interfere with the discovery process" (John-Steiner 1986, 86).

Georgia O'Keeffe, a scientist of art, demonstrated unusual feats of concentration, reaching into a flower or a landscape to represent its essence. Rudolf Arnheim, an adherent of the Gestalt approach who has written extensively about art, considered words secondary in shaping thought: "Language is essentially stabilizing and conservative."

The sculptor Henry Moore describes this process of creation as follows:

> I sometimes begin a drawing with no preconceived problem to solve, with only the desire to use pencil on paper and make lines, tones and styles with no conscious aim, but as my mind takes in what is so produced a point arrives where some idea becomes conscious and crystallizes, and then a control and ordering begins to take place.

Moore is describing a process that Jacob Getzels calls "Problem Finding" (Getzels and Csikszentmihalyi 1976). Getzels, a researcher at the University of Chicago, did a ten-year longitudinal study of beginning artists at a Chicago museum. He was interested in examining their thinking and concluded that problem finding was essential to the successful artist. Getzels writes:

The crucial step, one to which little attention has been paid, is how a situation where there is no problem to be solved gets transformed into a situation where a problem ready for solution exists. What needs to be examined is not only how artists solve problems they are already working on, but how they envisage and then formulate such problems in the first place. For the formulation of a creative problem is the forerunner of a creative solution.

Much of the work that children face in school involves problem solving. Generally, the teacher knows the solution beforehand and the child works to fulfill the assignment as accurately as possible. Although problem solving is important, it does not place the same demand on the child's thinking as problem finding. It is the blank page, the empty canvas, the workbench with tools and materials ready for work, the pottery wheel and lump of clay that require children to begin to *see differently*, to recognize a problem to be solved or an idea to be expressed. When the learner finds the problem, it is the learner as artist/scientist/inventor who can evaluate whether the problem has been solved or not. Words are important but represent only one part of a thinker's inner language. When we rule out the arts and other means of representing problems, we penalize a large number of our students. Equally disturbing, we thwart creative thinkers of the future, who come to see school as a false laboratory where they are required to fill in meaningless blanks on a page.

I return again to Georgia O'Keeffe and her desire to have her students learn to see beauty wherever it is found. She was a "problem finder" of the highest order, but she also exemplified the third and most important reason for art: beauty is an end in itself and needs no explanation. I see a beautiful vase and I am arrested by the wonder of it. Time stops. Past and future vanish. This vase exists now. Lewis Thomas, the noted neurophysiologist, writes: "Wonder comes from an ancient Indo-European root meaning simply to smile or laugh. Anything wonderful is something to smile in the presence of, in admiration (which, by the way, comes from the same root, along with of all telling words, *mirror*)" (Thomas 1983, 56). I look at the vase and I smile in its presence. I transcend time in a moment of pure joy.

79

Art and Children in the Classroom

Twenty-six years ago last spring, I was immersed in a study of seven-year-old children and their writing (Graves 1975). I sat next to children and recorded every change on their page, every conversation with other children, every use of resources or talk with the teacher. I noticed that children often drew before they wrote. Early in the study I waited patiently for the children to finish drawing. Michael, one of the case studies in the research, observed me pick up my pen and begin to write when he wrote. He liked the detailed attention I gave him, but one day he made a casual observation that changed the direction of my research. He said, "Know what, Mr. Graves? You like the writing, but I like the drawing."

I was surprised that Michael saw through my researcher's masquerade. He forced me to look at the business of self-expression through his eyes. At my next session I began to look at his process of drawing prior to writing. I placed the drawing and writing data side by side and charted the information in each (see Figure 9–1). Michael was correct in his judgment; in fact, there was much more information in his drawing than in his writing. On the chart, notice the empty spaces under the writing in relation to the drawing. Michael produces text for the beginning and end of what occurs in his drawing. The full episode he has drawn, the man falling in the water and the harpooning of the whale, is left out of the narrative. On the other hand, the text "They ate the blubber. It was good" is not in the drawing. It reflects the beginning of his transition from drawing into writing.

The data from this study show (Graves 1975) that the process of representation in children's art follows a rough sequence (see Figure 9–1).

Michael: Art and Writing Content—Composing Sequences
- One object drawn (a boat).
- Two objects appear (boat and sun).
- Two objects appear on water (beginning of setting for objects).
- Person appears in boat with bow and arrow, another boat approaches, figures are in profile facing interior. *This step usually contains the first depiction of motion or action. Narrative often begins at this point.*
- Narrative in drawing becomes more complex and filmlike in

Art (Prewriting Phase)		Writing (Composing Phase)	
ACTION	REACTION	ACTION	REACTION
1. "Whale drawn."	2. "Whale harpooned."	1. "Whale is by a ship."	2. "One man frew a harpoon at the whale."
3. "Fish and sun drawn."	_____	3. "One man is is reking a ship."	_____
4. "Whale strikes ship."	5. "Man falls into sea."	4. "One whale is rekin a ship."	5. _____
6. "Man swims in sea."	7. "Whale catches man."	6. _____	7. _____
8. "Paint spills on deck from whale striking boat."	_____	8.	
9. "New ship drawn. Man looks for whale."	10. "Man sees whale."	9. _____	10. _____
11. "Man drawn on deck."	_____	11.	
12. "Whale harpooned."	13. "Boat is lowered into water."	12. _____	13. _____
14. "Fake man is thrown into water to keep whale busy."	15. "Whale is shot with bow and arrow. Struck by 'thunder'."	14. _____	15. "It was raining fast. The fender hit the whale."
16. _____	17. _____	16. "They kill the whale."	17. "They ate the blubber. "It was good'."

Figure 9–1. Michael's art and writing content—composing sequences.

action/reaction couplets. *If writing accompanies the drawing, the drawing is often a rehearsal for what follows in writing.*

- Reduction of action/reaction couplets with only one or two unrelated events.
- Child chooses to represent one action from the text. *This is more like illustration and is done after the text is written.*

From the beginning children see art as representative of their inner and outer worlds. Their behavior resembles play: they talk to themselves while they compose, "And over here a guy is going to hit the deck cuz the whale hit the ship." Sound effects often accompany the actions represented on the page. We witness the prosodics of transition from the inner world to the outer world, from inner diagram and image to the discovery by the tongue and the recording by the hand of what is meaningful.

Notice the change in time/space dimension from the earliest depiction of a boat to the selection of one illustrated moment. The child must first discover time and narrative by moving hand and mind directly on the page, then gradually trim away the overdepiction into a significant narrative moment.

This is the essence of thinking. Yet it is not just the work of the artist. The scientist examines data trying to choose the hypothesis that explains the relationship of all the disparate variables. The writer pulls from thousands of options the living words, "We hold these truths to be self evident; that all men are created equal; that they are endowed by their Creator with certain inalienable rights; that among these are life, liberty and the pursuit of happiness" or "Fourscore and seven years ago our fathers brought forth on this continent a new nation conceived in liberty and dedicated to the proposition that all men are created equal." Lincoln picks up Jefferson.

Through the concrete world of art, children begin the lifetime process of making thoughtful choices. That process cannot end in first or second grade but must continue through all the years in school and throughout the curriculum. Children need large amounts of time to experiment without interruption. They need time to waste. It is up to us who have gone before them to point to the significance of their choices, to expect more. We provide the studio/laboratory for learning.

10

From Seeing to Art

The other day Betty and I were heading down the slope below our house on our way to do some clearing around a large tree we've named the Generation Oak. As I walked I calculated how far I would cut back on the hemlocks around the tree. I planned to stack the slash for burning with the first snowfall in early November. "Don, wait, look at this," Betty called from behind me on the trail. I turned and saw her pointing at a red-capped toadstool sitting amid some dark green star moss. The difference in colors (red against green) and textures (smooth and round shaped) against the delicate star-shaped moss was particularly beautiful.

"Yes, I know," I answered, as if I had casually had the same experience but hadn't bothered to tell her. I'd looked at the toadstool and the moss, but I hadn't seen them. There is a great difference between looking and seeing, as Georgia O'Keeffe reminds us. This chapter is about learning to see again.

We live in a noisy, busy world that shouts for our attention. We learn to screen out stimuli in order to perform the normal tasks of daily living. The problem is that we become accomplished at ignoring our senses. We look but we don't see.

Seeing is different from looking: in seeing we deliberately select from the environment. We place ourselves in a position to be affected by what is around us. If I were to walk down the hill again, I would allow myself to see what is there. Seeing is as essential to the artist and scientist as it is to the writer.

By pointing out the toadstool and the star moss, Betty reoriented me to the world around me. Sometimes we need to borrow the eyes of others, to "try on their glasses." It often takes people—our friends and family, characters in books, people we talk with—to see differently.

In *Photography and the Art of Seeing*, Freeman Patterson (1989) suggests that going to school is not going to help our seeing.

It was Monet, the painter, who said that in order to see we must forget the name of the thing we are looking at. When we are children we think primarily in pictures, not in words. But this approach is played down when we go to school. The basic analytical skills (reading, writing, and arithmetic) are impressed on us as being more important than the appreciation of direct sensory experience, so we come to depend less and less on the part of the brain that encourages visual thinking. . . . As Frederick Franck so aptly expresses it, "By these labels we recognize everything, and no longer see anything. We know the labels on the bottles, but never taste the wine."

I have to work at learning to see. I tend to be purpose oriented and to focus on carrying out some future plan.

ACTION: *Have children begin to discover what is beautiful inside the classroom as well as what is outside the classroom.*

This ACTION requires you to look hard. What you select may be part of an object, an article of clothing perhaps, a brooch, the repeated line in a vent, or the veined leaf of a geranium plant on the windowsill. This ACTION is like the one you did in Chapter 8 but it asks for more intense scrutiny.

This ACTION stresses what is "beautiful" as a beginning criteria, because finding something beautiful is a good entry point for children to begin to see. It is the seeing that is most important, rather than the finding something beautiful. Later, the children will look for what is grotesque. In both cases, children learn to resee the world around them.

I want to give the children some glimpse of the process of looking at objects. I talk aloud as I look around the room. I do want to demonstrate two principles: (1) the wholeness of an object, and (2) the way a part fits in and stands alone. I want children to recognize diverse criteria we have used for deciding something is worthy of notice. I expect the children to say things like

- "I liked the way it looked." *If the child gives this kind of global response say, "Touch the places where you liked what you saw." Sometimes it is just the feeling of a piece the child likes, and words fail. Touching may serve as a middle ground for expressing emotion.*

84

- "It has neat lines." *"Show me the lines you liked. Tell me what you see there."*
- "This has beautiful colors." *Possibly the colors are relational, an unusual blue book next to a red book.*
- "This has a nice shape." *"Show me with your hands how the shape goes."* (Note that I am tying one sense with another, the visual and the kinesthetic.)
- "I like this part here." *"I like the way you can see this small part out of the entire object."*
- "I like the way this feels, especially the two together, one feels this way, that one another way."

As the children talk, I make two lists, one of the objects they choose, and the other of the attributes they give them. Again, I want to stress the range and the variety.

After applying this ACTION inside the classroom, move outside and look for what is beautiful. Hold your sharing circle outside so children will be near their discoveries. You may also wish to have them bring something from home they consider beautiful.

ACTION: Choose an article to sketch, then draw it from different points of view.

You and the children may wish to choose something you have discovered at home, in the room, or outdoors. You may have to arrange for children to go outdoors. Have the children draw without taking their eye off the object or looking down at the page. Experiment with these questions, "Did you see anything different in your object when you sketched it? Was there anything new you didn't see before?"

This ACTION can be done individually or with a team of children. For example, a child may have brought in a model automobile from home to sketch. The object is to have the child sketch the auto from at least three vantage points in order to see how the appearance of the object changes. During sketching, have the children move to another spot or turn the object to create new angles of vision. Once again, children should draw rapidly, moving the pencil but not looking down at the paper. The point is to feel the shape and to discover with the eye what they may not have seen before they started to draw.

ACTION: Use cropping to isolate one part of a larger work.

Photographers often use this process when they look at large proofs that may not hold much promise. The photographer senses that there may be a smaller work embedded in the larger photo and tries cropping it to explore the picture. Cropping Ls are L-shapes made of heavy tag or the heavy stock used as display backing on bulletin boards. Figures 10–1 and 10–2 demonstrate this methodology. This exercise uses two sets of two sizes for working with large or small pictures: 5 by 3 by ½ inches and 10 by 6 by 1 inches. If larger Ls are needed, double the measurements.

I have taken the two L-shapes and turned them until I was able to put a temporary frame around the section of the larger photo I liked. The black rocks in the wall draw the eye to the cropped area, which did not happen when the larger photo stood alone.

It is often possible to discover a lovely work of art in a child's drawing that might otherwise be obscured by the elements around it. Cropping Ls are a valuable way for children to learn to select from a larger context.

I also use 3-by-5-inch cards with a small hole cut in the center in this process. Each child gets a card and I ask them to look for some things they find beautiful. Indeed, we might start with the classroom where we spend so much time from day to day. "Take your card and find some interesting objects or repetitions of lines or textures that you particularly like. Or, maybe there is a corner of the room or table that strikes you."

ACTION: Look for objects or areas that you consider grotesque.

Sometimes artists deliberately distort their work and place incongruous elements side by side in order to make a point. Viewers may be ill at ease in the face of such art, but that is the artist's intent. Victor Hugo, the nineteenth-century French writer, observed:

> Sublime upon sublime scarcely presents a contrast, and we need a little rest from everything, even the beautiful. On the other hand, the grotesque seems to be a halting-place, a mean term, a starting point whence one rises toward the beautiful with a fresher and keener perception. (Hjerter 1986, 23)

Figure 10–1. Snow scene along rock wall in woods

Figure 10–2. Cropping Ls placed on snow scene along rock wall

ACTION: Have the children begin to rank various areas in the room according to their aesthetic qualities.

In the previous ACTIONS, children have been learning to be observant as well as selective in their tastes. Consider now having them look at the classroom to choose the areas they feel are most pleasing to them aesthetically. You might ask them to select areas of grotesqueness as well. Obviously, there will be differences of opinion and these will provide important areas of discussion. There may be some surprising discoveries as well as some rethinking of the room structure. Above all, it will help the children to see where they live in a very different way.

As an option, have the children choose a place inside the school or even outside the school where people have worked to make an area more beautiful.

ACTION: Have the children interview a local artist, as I interviewed Juliette Hamelecourt, about the process of art and its connection to their lives.

Consider the questions I asked Juliette Hamelecourt. You may find that the art teacher at your school is a good interview choice. Or you may wish to interview a local artist who has exhibited; you may even be fortunate enough to schedule a visit to the artist's gallery and see examples of his or her work.

Final Reflection

We ask a simple question of those who serve as mentors, "What do you want?" Georgia O'Keeffe might respond, "I want to show my students a way of seeing. I want art to be something that everyone has to use. There is art in the line of a jacket and in the shape of a collar as well as in the way one addresses a letter, combs one's hair or puts a window in a house." Art is all around us if we stop, wonder, and see.

We want to travel with our children, to create beautiful objects of our own through sketching, painting, working with clay, collage, portrait, and in illustrating our stories. Learning to see, whether for reasons of aesthetics or science, is the most basic of skills. Seeing is at the heart of problem finding.

11

Science: Change in Motion

This morning as I write I am looking out the east window of my study at North and South Doublehead mountains. For the last two weeks I have watched fall come down the mountains. The maple, birch, and beech leaves first begin to change their colors at the highest elevations. In spring the process is reversed. Green appears in the valley and gradually works its way up the side until trees just below the summit of the mountain have leafed out.

On this October day, the leaves are near peak. The green chlorophyll has performed its summer duties remarkably. Like solar collectors, the leaf has brought in sunlight and fed the tree for four months. As sunlight lessens in late summer and fall, no more chlorophyll is made. The green maple leaf turns the bright red color it has worn all along underneath the green. As chlorophyll is used up beginning in late August, the tips of the leaf show flecks of red and throughout September gradually advance to bright red, then dark red. By the middle of October all the leaves will be on the ground.

Change is evident everywhere. This morning strong northwest winds with gusts to 45 miles per hour increased in strength as the warm sun encountered the cooler night air. We are reminded of change by the dawn, rising at the eastern base of North Doublehead at 5:26 A.M. in mid-June, now rising at 7:10 at the top of Middle Mountain, some thirty degrees to the south.

In tune with the season, the content of bear scat has changed from blackberry seeds to apple peel to beechnut and acorn hulls. The bears are in a hurry now to take in enough beechnut and acorns, which contain more fat than apples, to build up the layer of fat for hibernation. The female sow, in turn, must have enough fat to retain her fetus over the winter. In both fall and spring the pace quickens: first rapid growth, then the necessary work to survive the oncoming winter.

Science draws heavily on our verb repertoires. Whether our subject is biology, chemistry, physics, or geology, we enter the disciplines that attempt to explain the shifts in our universe from black holes to tectonic plates, from animal scat to the lessening of light and its effect on leaves.

This chapter is intended to open up your thinking about science by observing scientists, first the historic figure of Jean-Henri Fabre and later Dr. Bruce Hill, whose field of research is air pollution.

Jean-Henri Fabre

We enter the world of science through the great nineteenth-century French entomologist, Jean-Henri Fabre. I have chosen him for a particular reason. Before his time, science tended to describe final states; living things were studied for their anatomy and classified according to their proper phyla. James Clerk Maxwell, the great physicist who ranks next to Newton, transformed physics with his formulation of electromagnetic theory. Today, scientific investigation allows us to understand change in a very different way.

I look through Fabre's eyes at what he *wanted* as a scientist. I ask the question, "What was Fabre's deepest longing as a entomologist, as a person who wanted to study insects?" To understand his longing I begin with Fabre's early years and move to his systematic investigations. When I consider what a person wants I enter into the world of emotion and especially what drives the scientist conducting research.

Jean-Henri Fabre was born into extreme poverty in 1831 in Provence in the south of France. He was a dreamer and showed little interest in conventional studies, but he did teach himself to read from an alphabet chart of animals and insects his father brought home. To supplement the family earnings his father raised ducks, which became Fabre's responsibility. While he watched the ducks swimming in a small pond, he observed the insects surrounding the water habitat. Thus began his lifelong passion to understand the life cycles of living things in their habitats.

Fabre, showing some promise as a scholar, was admitted to the university, received his degree, and began to teach school. He continued poor, however, since he married and had a family that included five children. Somehow he managed to continue his observations and studies and eventually received a doctorate in natural sciences and a university appointment. His colleagues took advantage of him and stole the results of some of his experiments. He fell ill and was removed from his position, and only a chance relationship with the philosopher, John Stuart Mill, brought enough money to keep him alive. Even greater misfortune dogged Fabre, for his wife died as well as the son who served as his research assistant. At sixty he began life anew, married again, and had three more children, and began an unparalleled thirty-year stretch of research on insects in their natural habitats. His books are highly detailed and simply written. He longed to write for children of the next generation so that the magnificence of the insect world would not be lost.

I remember first reading about Fabre's work forty years ago in a biography, which noted that he created a living laboratory out of his own backyard. And what Fabre observed and recorded in that little backyard transformed entomology forever.

Fabre writes so eloquently and elegantly as he writes from his backyard. Notice how he comments on the rest of the field by commenting on his writing and scientific methodologies:

On Writing

Others again have reproached me with my style, which has not the solemnity, nay, better, the dryness of the schools. They fear lest a page that is read without fatigue should not always be the expression of the truth. Were I to take their word for it, we are profound only on condition of being obscure. Come here, one and all of you, the sting-bearers, and you, the wing-cased armour-clads—take up my defense and bear witness in my favour. Tell of the intimate terms on which I live with you, of the patience with which I observe you, of the care with which I record your actions. Your evidence is unanimous: yes, my pages though they bristle not with hollow formulas nor learned smatterings, are the exact narrative of facts observed, neither more nor less; and, whoso cares to question you in his turn will obtain the same replies.

And then, my dear insects, if you cannot convince those good people because you do not carry the weight of tedium, I, in my turn, will say to them:

"You rip up the animal and I study it alive; you turn it into an object of horror and pity, whereas I cause it to be loved; you labor in a torture-chamber and dissecting room, I make my observations under the blue sky to the song of the Cicadas, you subject cell and protoplasm to chemical tests, I study instinct in its loftiest manifestations; you pry into death, I pry into life.

And why should I not complete my thought: the boars have muddied the clear stream; natural history, youth's glorious study, has, by dint of cellular improvements, become a hateful and repulsive thing. Well, if I write for men of learning, for philosophers who, one day, will try to some extent to unravel the tough problems of instinct, I write also, I write above all things for the young. I want to make them love the natural history which you make them hate; and that is why, while keeping strictly to the domain of truth, I avoid your scientific prose, which all too often, alas seems borrowed from some Iroquois idiom."

Fabre spent his life trying to understand instinct in insects. This required hours and hours of observation out in the field. One story recounts how village women left town in the morning and ascended to the hills, baskets on their shoulders for harvesting grapes for making wine. One woman noted that she saw Fabre crouched down observing and recording the behavior of something on the ground. When she returned from the hill ten hours later, at day's end, Fabre held the same posture in the same location. In this instance, Fabre was studying the habits of the digger wasp, hoping he might see something new, some fragments he could combine with other fragments he had recorded. Fabre comments in a short piece, "Of Study and Observation":

> To collect these facts by fragments, to subject those fragments to varied tests in order to try their value, to make them into a sheaf of rays lighting up the darkness of the unknown and gradually causing it to emerge: all this demands a long space of time, especially as the favourable periods are brief. Years elapse; and then very often the perfect solution has not appeared. There are always gaps in our sheaf of light and always behind the mysteries which the rays have penetrated stand others, still shrouded in darkness.
>
> I am perfectly aware that it would be preferable to avoid repetitions and to give a complete story every time; but, in the domain of instinct

who can claim a harvest that leaves no grain for the gleaners? Sometimes the handful of corn left on the field is of more importance than the reapers' sheaves. If we had to wait until we knew every detail of the question studied, no one would venture to write the little that he knows. From time to time, a few truths are revealed, tiny pieces of the vast mosaic of things. Better to divulge the discovery, however humble it be. Others will come who, also gathering a few fragments, will assemble the whole into a picture ever growing larger but ever notched by the unknown.

I want to learn to think as a scientist thinks. Thus, to understand a scientist's thought more fully I approach Fabre as a character in a scientific drama. I ask a series of questions with which we have become familiar by now:

- What does Fabre want?
- How does Fabre set about getting what he wants?
- What are the tensions in his life?
- What ambiguities does he face and how does he deal with them?

From the outset, Fabre spent enormous amounts of time, often to the exclusion of all else, observing his insects. Indeed, poverty, a large family, and several jobs at once made it difficult for him to realize his ambition. Most people weren't interested in insects. He took that polarity and wrote about it. Because he placed the insect in context, little dramas emerged. Here is his description of two praying mantises at war with one another:

> For no reason that I can gather, two neighbors suddenly assume their attitude of war. They turn their heads to right and left, provoking each other, exchanging insulting glances. The "Puff! Puff!" of the wings rubbed by the abdomen sounds the charge. When the duel is to be limited to the first scratch received, without more serious consequences, the lethal fore-arms, which are usually kept folded, open like leaves of a book and fall back sideways, encircling the long bust. It is a superb pose, but less terrible than that adopted in a fight to the death.
>
> Then one of the grapnels, with a sudden spring, shoots out to its full length and strikes the rival; it is no less abruptly withdrawn and

93

resumes the defensive. The adversary hits back. The fencing is rather like two Cats boxing each other's ears. At the first blood drawn from her flabby paunch, or even before receiving the least wound, one of the duelists confesses herself beaten and retires. The other furls her battle standard and goes off else whither to meditate the capture of a Locust, keeping apparently calm, but ever ready to repeat the quarrel. (152)

Fabre wanted to investigate instinct, a nearly impossible task. He did what Henry Moore advised, "Everyone must have a goal and the goal must be high enough to be impossible to achieve." Of course, that is the paradox: as hard as Fabre tried, he never succeeded.

It is very difficult to be conclusive in the world of science. Why? What we know is always in motion. New knowledge always lies just around the corner. There is always the edge of discovery. Laws temporarily explain things, but soon there is paradox. Newton explained temporarily, then Maxwell with his theory of electromagnetism explained more. It takes unusual uses of time to understand change whether within people or the universe in which we live. Fabre observed, recorded, reflected, wrote, and did it again. If we are to understand how scientists think, we have to engage in scientific research. We have to do science in order to understand science. We have to become the students, working next to the people who do science in order to understand the world in motion. I need to look over the shoulder of scientists and see them observe the world and think about it. Although we may not be scientists, the children need us to be the people who look at the world of motion and show how we think. Further, as we invite them to observe with us, we observe as George O'Keeffe remarked, "I submit that if I give fresh eyes to my students, then I give still fresher eyes to myself. Imagine it, 31 sets of eyes all discovering anew." I believe, as David McCullough said about his students in history, that to engage in discovery is to provide an opportunity for our students to become emotionally involved with the subject, in this case science.

The ACTIONS in this chapter are designed to bring us inside the scientific experience. My emphasis will be on gathering data, reflecting, hypothesizing, and writing.

ACTION: Consider the changes going on around you.

Where there is change, there is often, but not always, movement. Often, where there is motion there is sound. This ACTION is just an opening to help us be aware of the place of science in our lives.

I sit at my computer to ponder where there is motion within my immediate vicinity. Some motion I can see, other motion I can hear, and then I can hypothesize about motion that I know is going on but can't see nor hear. I'll brainstorm a quick list:

- rain falling
- barometer needle falling
- tree and aspen leaves moving in southeast wind
- temperature moving on thermometer
- CD moving
- blade moving to blower in computer unit
- motor moving in my printer
- electrons moving in all my electrical equipment
- hand moving on computer keys
- air moving in my lungs
- blood moving through veins and arteries
- heart moving as it pumps
- bird feeder swaying in east wind
- juices moving in stomach
- material moving in gastrointestinal tract
- electrons moving as part of thought in brain
- feet moving beneath computer table
- mountains moving with upward thrust of geosyncline
- clock hand moving
- numbers changing on my digital watch
- water moving in brook
- birds flying in lower trees
- earth is moving in relation to sun as sun travels across sky from east to south, to west and setting.

Change is fascinating to the scientist and the artist. From my window I observe the afternoon light change on the face of North and South Doublehead mountains. Choose a place to sit, inside or outside,

95

and start to list everything that is moving around you. Using your senses: what you see, but also what you hear, what you feel.

ACTION: *Observe and record the shifts in light and shadow on the floor of a room.*

Take a piece of shelf paper and lay it out across the floor starting at a window where the sun shines in. Draw vertical lines on the shelf paper at one foot intervals. As the edge of the sun advances across the paper throughout the morning, record the time it touches each line. If your windows afford enough light, do the same during the afternoon. Although the sun "advances" on the paper, it is the rotation of the earth that is responsible for the perceived movement (see Figure 11–1).

I am fascinated by the position of the sun at various times of the year. During a year in Scotland, I tracked the sun along the chimney-pots on the houses across the green. Since we were in the northern latitudes, it cleared the chimneypot on one side at 9:45 A.M. in December, stayed about 3 degrees above the rooftop, and dropped from sight at 2:15 P.M., when the street lamps came on. The sun's angle also changes with the season (place the shelf paper parallel to the sun's rays and note the time).

ACTION: *Observe an animal or a pet for a period of twenty minutes on two separate occasions.*

Try to choose a time when you know your pet will be active, such as early morning, feeding time, or exercise time. The intent of this exercise is to record the animal's behavior. Researchers are interested in "what" data. Write down *what* you observe the animal doing. You may

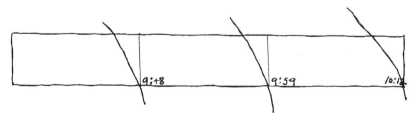

Figure 11–1. Sun in relation to earth rotation

notice a sequence and begin to hypothesize, to predict what the animal will do next. "I notice that just before my dog begins to eat, he looks around to see if there is anything that might disturb him, and then he plunges in."

I don't have a pet at the moment so I am observing an insect, a small cricket in a Mason jar habitat. It is October and we've had our first frost, so the insect population is somewhat diminished. Yesterday "Jimmy Cricket" was quite still, resting on some leaves. I rotated the jar to change the light and it began to crawl up a leaf but had difficulty going up the smooth leaf surface. In order to observe the cricket more closely, I took off the top of the jar. Quite suddenly, it jumped toward the opening but the jump was slightly off center and it struck the side.

This morning Jimmy is following the clear glass edges of the jar. It could be that the clear sides promise more liberation than the open top. Yesterday Jimmy was climbing up the leaf. Maybe the upward climb, the orientation "up," made him jump.

Later in the afternoon of my first observations I heard the sound of the cricket chirping. I quickly took off the cover of the jar and noted that the rear portion of the cricket fluffs out and shakes when it makes a noise. In all my years of hearing and observing crickets I'd never taken the time to observe one while it was chirping.

Of course, far more observation is needed. At the same time, scientists are constantly hypothesizing. The key is to be flexible and open to new data. When I hold to the particulars of a hypothesis with no ground or reason I am always curious to know why I *want* it to be so. Am I in a hurry? Or, am I thinking, "Well, if I were a cricket this is what I would do"? The longer we observe animals, the more we ascribe their behaviors as a result of our own value systems and patterns of acting.

ACTION: *Interview a scientist to discover how he or she thinks.*

Our subject disciplines should follow the contours of real people. You have had a chance to observe Jean-Henri Fabre. Now you will interview an actual scientist. I will do the ACTION with you. First, I need to think about scientists and where I might find them. Of course, it is a help when you happen to know anyone who does research. If you live near a university they are easy to find. Professors who deal with

97

the sciences—whether it's biology, chemistry, physics, agriculture—are usually engaged with research questions.

I don't live near a university so I had to look to extension services in agriculture or to those who might work with the environment. Quite often people in weather stations are doing research; or consider looking under the government listings in your telephone directory to locate someone working for the Environmental Protection Agency. You may find it helpful to look in the Yellow Pages and especially under governmental agencies. Many of them conduct research connected with science. If they aren't I suspect they would know people who were gathering scientific data.

This ACTION will be helpful to you as another ACTION appears in Chapter 12 in which you invite a scientist to your class so the children can learn how scientists think both personally and professionally. You may wish to invite the same scientist to your class whom you are interviewing for this project.

I am fortunate that one of my neighbors, Dr. Bruce Hill, is conducting research on the environment. To prepare for my interview I think ahead in two areas. You are already familiar with the first, character. That is, I look at what Bruce wants, the particulars of what he wants, the polarities this induces within himself and others and then at the nature of paradox as it applies to what he does and wants. The second part of my preparation involves understanding something about research.

All researchers have research questions that direct their work. These questions apply to research done in any discipline. In our area we have a problem with bears looking for food. If I were to conduct research I'd follow through on three research questions. My first research question is always *what: What do bears eat?* This is our old law of particularity. What are the details? What is the basic evidence that shows the details of what bears eat?

My second research question would be: How *do the eating habits of bears change?* Basically, I'm looking at *how* the *what* data change over time.

I know that when bears first come out of hibernation there is little to eat and they often rely on people's garbage, bird feeders, and so forth. The diet follows what is available in the growing season in this order: berries, apples, beechnuts, and acorns. Introduce droughts into the picture and bears have a tough time and turn again to people for sources of food. The latter observation now focuses on *why* bears may be destructive. Before I can answer a *why* question I must have the *what* and *how* data first. With my thinking about character and research questions, I move to my interview with Bruce Hill.

I ask a simple first question:

> Bruce, first let me tell you what I am doing and why I am here to interview you. I am writing a book in which there is a main focus on people and how they think. For example, if I want to understand the Declaration of Independence I need to see how Thomas Jefferson thinks, or I might want to interview a historian if I want to see how historians think. I'm interested in how you think as you do scientific research. Tell me what you do.

Bruce explains how the Appalachian Mountain Club, a large, environmentally oriented organization, first became involved in research under the leadership of his boss, Dr. Ken Kimball. They began to study acid rain and its effects and gradually moved to cloud moisture and smog.

> *Bruce:* My research is focused on air quality at high elevations and how this is related to public policy. I am looking at ozone smog and particle pollution. What I do is to monitor ozone at three levels from the top of the mountain (Mt. Washington) to the bottom. More specifically, I examine cloud rain chemistry. There is another monitoring station up by the Canadian border. Of course, stream chemistry is very closely related because atmosphere affects water quality. In addition we measure particle composition of the air and how it affects hikers.

Environmental scientists don't work in a vacuum. When they engage in their experiments they have an eye on their effects on the public at large and on the policy makers. Politics affects the source of funds that allow the scientists to do their work as well as the industries that may be required to lessen the pollution of their production. When Bruce works with policy makers, often lay people not well-informed in environmental science, he has to explain his data to make his points.

99

Don: I have a broad sense of your job as it works back and forth between actual research and environmental policy issues. I'd like you now to focus on a part of your research that interests you, to get a little closer to the science of your job. Choose one of the research questions that is close to your heart.

Bruce: OK, here's one: *Is visual haze caused by humidity or air pollution?*

Naturally, we have a bias, as most researchers do. Our hypothesis is that air pollution causes the haze. If we can get good data here we can begin to deal more effectively with some of the policy questions. Studying this has been a joint project working with the National Forest Service. So, simply put, what is it that causes the haze?

Don: Tell me about your design.

Bruce: We've greatly improved our techniques for gathering our data. In 1985 the Forest and Park service worked on this. They took photos three times a day on the North Presidential Range, in the Great Gulf, which is a Class 1 air shed. They came up with numbers on visibility and then applied a densotometer to the photos to determine quality.

In 1988 the Harvard School of Public Health came up with a procedure in which you'd capture air and whatever was there would be caught in a filter. These are extremely small particles that will be caught down to a millionth of a meter.

So then, there's another research question here: *Does the visibility decrease as the particles increase?* How significant is this and how is it connected to humidity? We preweighed the particles and postweighed them.

We dug into the literature and it helped us to realize that hypothetically when there is sulfur in the atmosphere, the sulfur will grow in the presence of moisture. In short, there is a synergistic relationship between humidity and particles. The particles are made up of nitrogen oxide, ammonia, and sulfur. Over half of the particles are sulfur, which is the product of combustion. Of course, the acidity of the particles affects the rain.

We saw that the pollution level at high altitudes was the same as in the cities. Another study got us involved here, in that Brigham and Women's Hospital in Boston studied the effect on hikers at higher elevations. The results of their study are just coming out in a National Medical Journal.

I am getting a good sense of how Bruce thinks about his design and data but I am curious about some of the personal issues here that may be related to his pursuit of research.

Don: As a researcher you must have some walls or difficulties that you encounter as you try to reach your objectives. Sometimes the walls are within and sometimes they are without. Would you comment on this?
Bruce: Yes, I have some bargains to make with how I use my time. I can't predict when I'll suddenly have to go to Washington for meetings with congressional and regulatory agencies. Fortunately, I have two hired interns to help keep the research going.

Mostly, we monitor during the summer. From April to October are the heavy data-gathering months; from November through March, public planning sessions.
Don: So what bugs you?
Bruce: What really bugs me is the constant struggle for support. Foundations are looking for flashy stuff, real grassroots stuff. They want quick results: Does the law make a difference in one to three years? The problem is that there is great variability in the meteorology, so short-term stuff doesn't work. You could have two dry years in the three-year monitoring term that would show poor data. Anything involving climate is automatically long-term.

Frankly, long-term research can get boring. You have to keep your monitoring going gathering very repetitive data. There's a tedium to it.
Don: You are more like a private detective sitting in a car waiting days and days for the person you are observing to do something significant.
Bruce: Yes, sort of like that. It is like preparing for a marathon. You train and train putting your time in. Finally, something significant comes from it.

There's, of course, the bright side to this. The day I sat next to the EPA lawyer and I could bring all my science to bear on an important question was very, very satisfying.

Oh, there's another one that bugs me. Of course, in research there's always the next question, there's always more data to be brought in, which is what the cigarette companies argued for years even though they were lying through their teeth because they had data in their possession that proved nicotine was addictive. Industry preys on this.

101

They keep arguing, "We need further research." These guys are big-time lawyers with huge budgets behind them. The lobbies behind them are huge too.

The battle is often lost with the media as well. They grab the simple data or one simple statement from industry, "We need more data," and that becomes the news of the day.

In reviewing the interview I note that Bruce's wish to raise air quality standards immediately puts him up against hostile forces. How does he maintain data gathering over many years? How will he get funding to sustain his research? With research that must run climactic cycles long-term how will he sustain it personally and acquire the money he needs to see the research through to completion? While all this is going on how will the data he gathers have the true effect that is his main want, to improve the environment? The paradox is that the world doesn't hold still. Change is constant, yesterday's data can grow old before it can have its desired effect.

Final Reflection

Science helps us to understand a physically changing world. The psychologist Jerome Bruner (1990) and Vera John-Steiner, a psycholinguist (1985), have shown us that if we are to learn in various disciplines, but particularly in the sciences, we need to be near those who do science and to observe how they formulate questions about the world and then follow those questions to an answer or a solution. Children must experience research firsthand: a sense of discovery is essential to scientific inquiry and helps our children to experience the emotions that make science an important and delightful study.

12

Learning to Think
Through Science

A few years ago I was observing children learning to read and write in Leslie Funkhouser's second grade classroom in Lee, New Hampshire. In the spring, Leslie got duck eggs from the university poultry farm and the loan of an incubator with a guide about temperature control. They had a rough idea when the ducklings might hatch and kept charts on any shifts they observed in the eggs. Leslie's students were engaged in scientific thinking.

The excitement grew when the eggs first began to rock and then a bill appeared, until each of the ducklings emerged. Food and water were placed in the little pen with lightbulbs in the corners to maintain the proper temperature. Meanwhile, the children kept careful records on eating habits, food consumption, the appearance of feathers. I marveled at the quality of the children's engagement as they used their records to hypothesize about the lives of these ducks.

About eight days after the ducklings had hatched, on a Monday morning, Leslie and the children came in and immediately spotted serious trouble. Three of the ducklings were hardly moving, and those that were moving were having trouble maintaining their balance. Leslie quickly called the children over to the rug and in her usual frank manner said, "Children, I don't know what the trouble is, but if we don't get busy, these ducklings are going to die." Leslie asked the most basic question: "Why are the ducks sick?"

Curious but anxious, the children sallied forth, determined to save the ducklings. Some went to the library to see Mrs. Taft, the librarian. "We've got to find books to save our ducklings." A few went to the office to call the university. One child asked to visit Mrs. Damon, the kindergarten teacher. "She has ducks, Mrs. Funkhouser. Maybe she can help us."

By recess, the children had returned from their information-gathering expeditions, and the child who went to the kindergarten returned with Mrs. Damon. Mrs. Damon took one look at the ducklings and the pen and made an immediate diagnosis. "Look what you are doing to the ducklings. That water dish is the problem. You see, at first these ducklings have no natural oil to protect them, and they've probably got pneumonia or a very bad cold." Mrs. Damon carefully toweled off the ducklings and took them down to the warming ovens in the cafeteria. In short order, the ducklings recovered and safely returned to the classroom.

At the class meeting, Leslie apologized to the children. "Gracious," she said, "I'd always thought that ducks liked water, and I never realized that the water dish was a problem." They discussed what they should have done and were thankful that Mrs. Damon's expertise saved the day.

Although near trauma was attached to their explorations the children were successfully engaged in observing change firsthand. They measured, recorded, observed many of the changes that went with ducklings entering the world. Science is a verb culture in which children need to experience firsthand shifts and growth in living things. Discovery and wonder is the heart of any discipline. However small, authorship is the first cousin of discovery. "Come over here and look what I've found, Ms. Funkhouser" is an indication of discovery and the beginning of scientific authorship.

ACTION: *Make a list of things that move right in the classroom.*

1. Make a list of what you can see that is moving. (Remember, for example, that the sun causes shadows and light to move, etc.)
2. Make a list of what you hear. (Sounds come from things that are moving.)
3. Make a list of what moves that you can't see. (My chest goes up and down when I breathe. Blood moves through my veins and arteries. Water is moving in the pipes. Air is moving in the room.)

You may wish to take this ACTION outdoors. Take a soft ball of clay or anything soft (play-dough, bread dough, etc.) and throw the ball at a pile of sand. Examine the ball and the sand. How have they changed? Which of these two objects do you think was affected most and why? Which one is more durable? Apply this idea in other contexts:

- Tires meeting the road
- Clothing hung on a hook
- Saw cutting wood
- Pencil on a piece of paper

Elicit other objects that meet and interact to discuss how both are changed. Apply the concept of the more durable substance as the one possibly receiving the least change. Be sure to note that though one substance is very hard change still occurs in that object.

Ask the children to hypothesize about which will change more and why.

ACTION: *Chart the motion of the sun on paper.*

Draw squares on a six-foot piece of white paper, as you did in the previous chapter. Place the paper so the edge of the sun will light up on one side of the paper and move across it. Mark off vertical lines at three-inch intervals and follow the edge of the sun as it moves across the paper. The earth is rotating as it moves around the sun; show children how to estimate how long it takes the sun's light to move from square to square.

ACTION: *Choose a plot of land to examine regularly throughout the school year.*

This ACTION echoes the work of Jean-Henri Fabre. Observing lends itself to a wide range of data gathering and hypothesizing. Even more valuable is the demonstration of how various aspects of field science interact: changing weather, the season, the amount of light, the length of days all affect the relationships between residents and growing things.

The ideal place for a plot of land is right on the school grounds. Many schools are not built on prime real estate, which means that school surroundings may be more rugged than usual. I like tangled undergrowth, trees and shrubs, and a range of vegetation. This allows more firsthand observation. If you cannot observe a plot on the grounds, perhaps a neighbor within walking distance will allow children to visit the yard. Of course, the intention is to study, not to harm the land in any manner.

Vegetation will provide habitat for organisms that live off the leaves and grasses: crickets, grasshoppers, aphids, Japanese beetles, worms, beetles, mice, voles, chipmunks, and squirrels as well as all kinds of bird life.

I'd suggest a twenty-by-twenty-foot plot (but even a ten-by-ten-foot plot is adequate). You may wish to mark off the boundaries with stakes or string. If possible, have the class participate actively in choosing it.

- Note changes in shrubs, grasses, and trees as seasons progress. I like to choose one leaf to watch, beginning with the first tassel or green bud on a tree to full leaf in spring. I do the same in the first week of September or when I see the first bit of color.
- Note changes due to drought, snow, or rainfall.
- Consider placing a rain gauge on the plot. You can make your own by taking a clear plastic bottle and marking off even levels with ink.
- If you live in snow country, mark a stake at one-inch intervals and record the amounts of snow on the chart. Note the changes in frost level in the ground in late fall or early spring by digging in one location to note the depth. Record earth temperatures by placing a thermometer in the soil. This is especially useful in spring in making a connection between soil temperature and growing things.
- Have children map out vegetation on the plot and identify it. Note any small tree seedlings.
- Note what may be decaying.
- Note any insects and identify them. Where possible, allow time for observing insects or any crawling thing.
- If birds rest on the plot note what they do and what they eat.
- If possible, put up a bird feeder.

You may find it possible to keep foot traffic to a narrow path down the middle of the plot so that children may observe left and right without disturbing anything.

My attitude toward the land is one of great respect, unlimited curiosity, and wondrous anticipation. Curiosity is fed by careful records, sketches, photos, and paintings. Journals recording day-by-day observations and noting changes are helpful.

ACTION: *Purchase two pumpkins in early September (preferably green) and observe the change in color (green to orange) through to final decay.*

This observation works especially well with kindergarten and primary-school children. I recall one class that named the pumpkin "Rotten Jack." The process of decay is fascinating: shape, color, and odor all change over time. The children draw, photograph, and write in their journals. Discuss these changes in light of other kinds of decay in the world. Why do things decay? Suppose they didn't?

Your role as teacher is to think aloud and to ask questions. Of course, the most important questions of all come from the children.

"Why does it smell?"

"Why is it starting to fall in?"

Rub one of the two pumpkins with bleach periodically to retard decay. Compare the two pumpkins. You may wish to weigh them at the start and record weight shifts. "Where does all the weight go?"

ACTION: *Observe a pet or any animal over time.*

- What does the animal do?
- How does the animal do it?
- Why does the animal do it that way? (This is where children learn to hypothesize.)

For household pets I try to observe the animal at the same time or doing the same things every day: eating, playing with a favorite toy, going outside for exercise, asking to come in, or when visitors ring the doorbell.

The challenge is to observe as many different kinds of behavior as possible without making any judgments. Wonder is an important and exciting part of observation. Figure 12–1 records my observations of my dog at feeding time.

DOG DOES	I DO	I WONDER
	Turn crank to open can of dog food.	
Dog comes in from the other room.		Does the dog smell the food or does the dog know the sound of the can opener?
Dog dances. Eyes look up at me. Gives short bark.		Is this the same look she gives me when she wants to go outside?
	Put dish of dog food down next to water bowl.	
Dog moves back so I can put the bowl down.		
Dog looks around the room. Dog looks up at me.		Is the dog looking to see if someone might come to take the food away?
Dog begins to eat, eating meat pieces first.		Why does the dog select the best food first?
Dog eats rapidly, tag makes jingling noise on side of bowl.		
Eating seems to slow as she gets near the end of food left in bowl.		I wonder if she will eat it all, clean up every scrap, or end by licking the bowl.
Dog leaves a few grains of bits in bowl.		
Dog goes into living room and lies down under table.		I wonder if the dog will sleep now.

Figure 12–1: Observation of dog eating

Children need the most help in recording behavior. Replaying a video again and again gives them good practice in learning to see.

ACTION: Consider a study of fall leaves.

This particular study is directed at experimentation. Much of what we've been doing to this point might be called descriptive. If you compared the two pumpkins but then introduced bleach, you have moved from descriptive to experimental research.

"I wonder why" is the beginning of good science. If emotional involvement leads children to science, as a teacher I want to demonstrate a methodology that satisfies that wonder. I consider these steps:
1. A question: "I wonder why leaves change color."
2. Think aloud or do some reading about what affects leaves (for example, light, rainfall, temperature).
3. Consider ways to control light, rainfall, and temperature. For example, dig up three small tree seedlings from the wild with leaves about eighteen to twenty-four inches high, place them in pots, and control the amount of water, light, and temperature. Or put bags around leaves to retard light to see if this affects chlorophyll.
4. The next question: "How do these data relate o each other or change over a time?" (I'm hoping I will be able to say, "This is *why* leaves change. This is the truth at which I have arrived.")
5. Have children move into teams to think through how they will record the information they gather.

ACTION: Demonstrate to children through a "think-aloud" how you will consider writing up the data about leaves.

Children need to see how to write up a science experiment and what kind of thinking goes into writing. Researchers try to explain their data so that other scientists can replicate their findings. Here is sample dialogue (the actual written text is in italic):

Teacher: OK, we've finished gathering our information. We need to show where all this started. That's where we'll begin to write. Any ideas?

109

Child: When the leaves start to turn?

Teacher: But what made us decide we ought to start gathering information on the changes in the leaves in the first place?

Child: I think someone came in with some of those swamp maple leaves, which were very red. And you said, "How did this leaf get to be red?"

Child: And we didn't know why.

Teacher: Let's stop right there.

> *One day in September we were on a field trip and Mr. Graves asked us why some leaves were green and others were turning red. We didn't know, so we did a little reading (cite books) and found out that probably water, especially sunlight, and temperature all had something to do with the leaves turning color.*

Teacher: The next thing we'll do is show how we set the whole thing up. That's the next thing we set out to do. I'll call that "Design."

> *Design: We decided to go and find some small maple seedlings about 18″ high and put them in pots. When we got them they all had green leaves. We controlled for water, light, and temperature. This chart shows what we did for each of our potted trees.*

	Temperature	*Water*	*Light*
Pot 1	*Keep outdoors*	*2 cups every 2 days*	*Fully open to outside*
Pot 2	*Keep outdoors*	*1 cup every 2 days*	*Gauze over leaves*
Pot 3	*Keep indoors*	*1 cup every 4 days*	*Only natural house light*

Teacher: The next thing you will do is turn to your journals and write about each of the pots. You'll want to check your drawings to see where the red first came into the leaves. Write what you saw and how the leaves changed over the six weeks from September to the middle of October.

Finally, you will write your conclusion, which involves comparing the pots at the very end. Each of these steps will probably need several rewrites. When the scientist visits our class, you may want to ask about writing things up.

Children need to watch you go through the process, talking aloud to give them some picture of the kinds of thinking as you both write and design the study. You will be composing right along with them as you write up the results of each pot as well as your final conclusions about showing the results of your study. Of course, it is not always easy to control things just the way you'd like. Controlling water outside may mean controlling light as well. You have but one pot indoors to control for temperature. Things can go wrong there as well. The most important thing is that you and the children together are developing a process of thinking about science.

ACTION: *Interview a scientist.*

The person the class interviews ought to be engaged in some kind of data gathering. The purpose of the interview is twofold: to learn how scientists think and to understand why people are engaged in practicing science. It is important for the children to practice interviewing beforehand. Consider in advance the kinds of questions that will yield the information they wish to have.

In my preliminary interview, I look for someone with a passion for the subject. As I mentioned in earlier, most universities or counties, or governmental agencies such as the Environmental Protection Agency, food inspectors, or persons working in pest control, have a scientific stance toward their work.

The following questions are helpful in conducting the interview. Remember, you want children to get a feel for how scientists gather information and think about what they are doing.

- What do you do?
- How come you do that? What got you started?
- What excites you about what you are doing?
- What do you wonder about?
- What's hard about it?
- How did you prepare yourself to do what you are doing now?

I often role-play a scientist so we can rehearse before children actually interview an invited guest. The best questions, of course, are the follow-up questions the class asks that are based on the information the scientist gives. I have written more extensively on helping children learn to interview in *Investigate Nonfiction* (1987, 72–76). For teachers working in the primary grades who want to learn more about interviewing, I especially recommend Paula Rogovin's *Classroom Interviews in Action* (1998). She has built an entire curriculum on the interview alone.

Final Reflection

The world is in a constant state of change. Children need to get up from their desks to explore and discover the wonders that are waiting for them.

Change is only understood as a durational concept. If I want to understand the movement of the earth, I observe how the earth changes in relation to the sun on a piece of paper. If I want to understand insect or animal behavior I must record intervals of their behaviors. Discovery and wonder occur when we see the change phenomena in relation to what has come before our immediate observations.

The true scientist is constantly wondering about the world and asking questions to try to understand and explain it. The emotional rewards of science are closely connected to scientific inquiry. Children need to observe and wonder. They also need to encounter adults who are passionately engaged in their work. This is the kind of human encouragement that jump-starts learning.

13

Bring Life into Learning

A short time ago, Roger Mudd interviewed the historian David McCullough on the History Channel. McCullough got on to the subject of teaching history at Cornell. "I'm not satisfied until my students fall in love with history." He deliberately structured learning toward discovery. Each student received an artifact: a photo, a playbill, a letter, or a piece of sheet music. These artifacts served as windows through which students could view an entire period of history. They inevitably led to people who lived during important events of an era.

The process of discovery inspires a sense of wonder. McCullough's observations could be applied to any subject or discipline children may study. Wonder's friend is time. If I am rushing to cover a subject or prepare for an examination before children have understanding, I waste their time. Worse, without realizing it, I may be teaching them a needless aversion to a beautiful and important area of study.

Think back to the life of Georgia O'Keeffe. Her great concern was to take time to look at the world and to see it differently. She took long walks in Amarillo, Texas, sometimes alone, but sometimes with her students. Her students could see the world differently through her eyes.

In *Notebooks of the Mind*, Vera John-Steiner points out the importance of immersion, of being lost in a "sea" of deep thought. It is a common characteristic of important thinkers. In his book *Flow*, Mihaly Csikszentmihalyi (1990) shows the importance of concentration, of becoming lost in a subject. Immersed in a subject, our emotions are heightened. Irrespective of disciplines, the people who have appeared in this book focused for long periods on one area of investigation. Their sense of wonder kept them so focused, time literally disappeared.

In our classrooms, however, we are programmed to small slots of time punctuated by interruptions. We focus on the tools of learning at the expense of learning itself. When a teacher has only a fifteen- to twenty-minute block of time, spelling, math facts, or phonics are what fit. There is an unfortunate relationship between interpreting small paragraphs or the skill assessment sections of standardized tests and the slot-based nature of classroom time. Consider how absurd it would be if carpenters were trained to build houses by having daily instruction in the following curriculum:

9:00–9:15	Hammer instruction
9:15–9:30	Plane instruction
9:30–9:45	Instruction in use of power screwdriver
9:45–10:00	Instruction in use of the chisel

Under this curriculum, student carpenters wouldn't have time to build homes on the job. Carpenters do need to know how to use tools and children should become proficient in reading and spelling, but what is missing are the long stretches of time required for children to lose themselves in applying the tools. When the child is emotionally engaged in a subject, the tools become the unseen means to acquiring and applying knowledge.

The smaller the time for learning, the more the teacher initiates instruction: "All right, children, clear your desks and take out your spelling books." And for every transition, there is the wasted time of taking down one learning activity and setting up another.

Teachers understandably argue, "But children have such short attention spans, twenty minutes seems to be all the time they can handle on their own." On the contrary, the average child in America watches forty-five hours of television a week. Although the programming is not the best, the more serious danger television poses is the erosion of self-motivated playtime. I would ask these questions: "What is the quality of playtime when the TV set is turned off? What is the child *initiating* through constructions, games, reading, and the like?"

TV provides external motivators, whereas play is a self-made, self-motivated activity. In play, the child chooses materials or activities and pursues them toward a chosen end. At the same time, the child is his own self-evaluator. "I like this, I don't like that; I'll do more of this and less of that." The child who plays for long periods of time is the child who will also be emotionally engaged in learning at school. Good play is the foundation of lifelong learning.

Ken Dryden, the all-time professional hockey player who has written one of the most intelligent books on sport and society (*The Game*), laments the programming of young children to become superior athletes, students, persons:

It all has to do with the way we look at free time. Constantly preoccupied with time and keeping ourselves busy (we have come to answer the ritual question "How are you?" with what we apparently equate with good health, "Busy"), we treat non-school, non-sleeping, or non-eating time, unbudgeted free time, with suspicion and no little fear. For, while it may offer opportunity to learn and do new things, we worry that the time we once spent reading, kicking a ball, or mindlessly coddling a puck might be used destructively, in front of TV, or "getting into trouble" in endless ways. So we organize free time, scheduling it into lessons—ballet, piano, French—into organizations, teams, and clubs, fragmenting it into impossible-to-be-boring segments, creating in ourselves a mental metabolism geared to moving on, making free time distinctly unfree.

It is in free time that the special player develops [*I would add thinker*], not in hour-long practices once a week, in mechanical devotion to packaged, processed, coaching-manual, hockey-school skills. For while skills are necessary, setting out as they do the limits of anything, more is needed to transform those skills into something special. Mostly it is time—unencumbered, unhurried, time of a different quality, more time, time to find wrong answers, to find a few that are right; time to find your own right answers; time for skills to be practiced to set higher limits, to settle and assimilate and become fully and completely yours, to organize and combine with other skills comfortably and easily in some uniquely personal way, then to be set loose, trust, to find new instinctive directions to take, to create. (1984, 135)

For the various thinkers and artists mentioned in this book or for anyone who achieves, time alone to pursue their own thoughts and constructions has been a necessity. Although children come to school less and less able to handle time alone, at school we tend to reinvent the unpredictable pattern of home behavior that renders the child disconnected from learning. Gordon Wells' (1986) distinguished study of patterns of learning at home and school shows the importance of story reading and sharing at home in children's literacy. Sadly, children who have not had experienced reading aloud at home tend to receive skill drills in school, yet another replication of learning that doesn't work. They are deprived of the intimacy of story, the feeling of human closeness, the drama of human adventure.

Changing Direction

The ACTIONS in this book have invited you to rediscover the people around you. You have helped children to discuss the characters in their books whose choices often parallel those in children's lives.

You have helped children to see the world differently. The children have observed, sketched, role-played, tried on other personalities, read, and written, all with a view to understanding the world of history or science. If you have done these things, you began to use time differently. You reached for larger blocks of time. You began to make decisions about cutting curriculum for the sake of learning.

Instinctively, you've always known that without an emotional attachment to learning, lasting learning simply doesn't happen. Think back to your own experience from grade four through college. Perhaps a few meaningful learning episodes stand out that you remember with the joy of intense engagement.

Children need to *feel* the points of view of rebels and Tories to understand the complexities of the American Revolution. It is in the record keeping and observation of changes in the land that children encounter the *feeling* of wonder about the rhythms of seasons, and the interrelationships and balance of nature. The children could feel what it meant to know a subject well when they interviewed experts.

You have learned that inviting all kinds of children into learning takes time and careful orchestration. Your initial investment of energy is high as you read, write, gather materials, and line up human resources from the various disciplines. But the energy comes back to you in the wonder and affirmation in the children. It may seem like slow going at first, but once children follow their wonder, the pace of their learning and their retention increase. You've known the power of wonder for years because you've experienced it in your own life. You may not have experienced it in school, but nearly everyone can identify something they know how to do well and recall how they learned it. Chances are you were attracted by someone who could practice the skill. They painted, danced, cooked, gardened, restored old furniture, collected old bottles, rebuilt golf clubs, fished, cycled, or skied. You caught a vision of fulfillment in the deftness with which your mentor worked. You experimented with one small aspect, felt some success and some failure, but in your first small achievement you caught a vision of the possible. You were hooked. At first you dabbled and your investment of time was small, but as your involvements became greater, your emotional investment returned a hundredfold.

We have also known the boredom of sitting while teachers talked and talked about what we needed to know. They tried to tell us about the excitement of learning instead of helping us experience it. We remember answering questions at the end of a history chapter or filling in the worksheets on science experiments that were supposed to turn out a certain way. We went into teaching vowing that our students wouldn't be bored, that learning would be exciting. Holding a vision of how engaging learning could be, we sallied forth.

We have gradually seen our vision dimmed by the weight of curriculum, the small blocks of time, constant interruption, and the layers of paperwork at the local, state, and national level. It seems that every politician in America wants to know how we are doing because they don't trust themselves or us to do the job properly. And the lack of trust depletes our energy. Secretly, we suspect that distrust has dulled our freshness. We see a certain lifelessness in the quality of our children's engagement. Listen to Stephen Cary's experience, reported in *How to Help English Learners:*

> Toward the end of a recent workshop in the East Bay, one of the central office administrators popped in and asked me to take a few moments to summarize my nine years of consulting work in the public schools. She wanted an "overall impression" of what I'd seen as a teacher coach hopping classroom to classroom around California. What had I learned about the public schools after observing in over fifty districts?
>
> I told the group of K–12 teachers that I didn't need much time to synthesize my impressions; I could sum up my experiences in three

words. The room grew quiet. Even the knitters, doodlers, and paper graders pushed aside their work and gave a listen. After the requisite dramatic pause, I dropped the bomb: "School is boring." I sat down. There was dead silence for a few seconds, then the room erupted in applause. Heads nodded their agreement. Many in the audience offered a corroborative "Yeah!" or "That's right!"

I've been dropping the same little three-word bomb whenever I get the chance for a couple of years now. Everybody always applauds. It's the applause of recognition. Teachers are bright folks. They know school isn't engaging. It's tedious and often painful, but only rarely is it exciting and relevant. They know most of what goes on in school is not real, not authentic. Teachers know deep down in their bones that marching kids year after year through skill-driven activities drained of content and emotion only makes sense if our goal is a skilled citizenry, not a skilled and thinking, creative citizenry.

They know that. Teachers know that. They even applaud when someone like me in a blue blazer and a tie drops in from Consulting Land and reminds them that they know that. And yet, still, school is boring. Brain-dead, flatlined boring. I remain an optimist, nevertheless, and continue to pray daily to the God of Rich Content. She must be taking a really long nap. (Forthcoming)

A Majority of One

We know the source of our energy as well as what depletes it. For ourselves and our children we appoint ourselves a majority of one to shift our professional direction. The most important character in all of this is you, the teacher.

The children study you from the moment you enter the classroom in the morning until you leave in the afternoon. You buy a new auto, dress, or briefcase and the news travels swiftly throughout the room. They are interested in what you *want*. They want to feel what you feel passionate about—a book, a current event. They wonder how you learn and what you do when things don't work. The children who struggle have a history of things not working; they wonder what you do when things go wrong. They watch and learn.

Above all, they rely on your energy and how you create energy within them. They realize as you do that when you believe in them and note their smallest improvements they feel the energy of wanting to learn more.

My new commitment to professionalism requires me to know my subject better than before. I will have studied it in greater depth and now decide which elements of curriculum must be deleted and what will be kept. Professionalism requires me to say yes to some things and no to others. I say no to inflated curriculum that forces me to bypass children, and I say yes to high quality curriculum that allows the children to discover subjects for themselves. It is my openness to all learning that allows me to help children to discover subjects I have not discovered. I am able to recognize and celebrate the children's small victories, and that gives them energy.

Finally, I say no to fragmented time, which replicates learning disconnected from people, and say yes to longer stretches of time that allow for discovery, for the energy of wonder that fuels the children as it fuels my new professionalism. I commit myself to bring new life to learning and new learning to life.

ACTIONS

Chapter 2: A Workshop on People

- *ACTION: Choose a person you know well and list the ways in which she reveals herself.*
- *ACTION: Write a short paragraph about the person you have described showing that person in a familiar situation.*
- *ACTION: Take ten minutes to do a quick written sketch of a person you do not know.*

Chapter 3: Learning to Read Characters

- *ACTION: Consider each of the characters in "The Boy and the Moose."* As an option, try this ACTION with a partner. Compare and contrast your understanding of the characters. Try this ACTION by following these steps in the recommended sequence.
  1. Without looking back at the text, note what you think each of the following characters in the story *wants:* Edney, father, mother, moose, Mr. Huckaby.
  2. Now turn back to the story and reread it. As you read, try to identify the characters' internal and external conflicts.
  3. Which struggles interest you the most? The least? Why?
  4. Try to recall any thoughts elicited by the text that have no connection to the actual story.
  5. Call the partner who has agreed to carry out this ACTION with you. Compare what you have discovered about yourselves as readers, and your thinking about the story, in the first four steps.

Chapter 4: A Reading and Writing Workshop on Character

- *ACTION: Conduct a series of workshops with your students in which they begin to learn about characters and the other necessary ingredients that go into fiction.*

- ACTION: *Use children's own reading books to demonstrate how writers introduce their characters.*
- ACTION: *Help children to develop characters in sharing sessions or small-group workshops.*
- ACTION: *Conduct a workshop on naming characters.*
- ACTION: *Select photographs from newspapers or magazines, mount them on tag paper, and use them to show children how to do quick word sketches.*

Chapter 5: Constructing Ourselves

- ACTION: *Look back at the characters you created in Chapter 2. Examine their traits and consider how you might shift your portrayal in a positive or a negative way.*
- ACTION: *Choose a short section of text from a book or magazine you have never read before and record what goes through your mind while you are reading it.*

Chapter 6: People and History

- ACTION: *Using the outline on page 39, consider what you can apply to an understanding of the character of Jefferson as well as the signing of the Declaration of Independence.*
- ACTION: *Choose an individual central to an important decision in history or current affairs. Write one paragraph giving background, a second paragraph showing what that person wanted to achieve, and a third paragraph showing the complementary or antithetical relationship between personal desires and historical outcomes.*
- ACTION: *Interview a historian to learn how that person approaches the subject.*

Chapter 7: Opening New Doors to History

- ACTION: *Experiment with drama to introduce the children to the people involved with the Declaration of Independence.*
- ACTION: *Experiment with group role playing to help children experience history as a group.*
- ACTION: *Demonstrate on the overhead how to write a letter.*
- ACTION: *Interview a local historian or someone who has lived through or knows about a particular event you may be studying.*

Chapter 8: Artful Thinking

- ACTION: *First, choose a room or some location familiar to you. Next, choose ten objects there that are pleasing to you, that you consider beautiful. Finally, write about why you consider three of these objects beautiful.*

- ACTION: *Choose an object that is pleasing to you. Draw it once to see it anew. Take a clean piece of paper and draw it a second time, as if you had never seen it before. Draw the object a third time from memory.*

- ACTION: *Choose an object that interests you. Continue to sketch it until your study of line and texture reveal something new to you.*

- ACTION: *To Georgia O'Keeffe bones represented the desert. Look for an object that captures the essence of a place. Begin to sketch it and evaluate it: "yes, good choice," or "no, bad choice." In this ACTION you are reaching to explore this object in relation to a broader context.*

- ACTION: *Who do you go to when you have finished creating something? Write for five minutes about why you choose that person. Or, write a short letter telling them why you go to them.*

- ACTION: *Interview a working artist to begin to appreciate how artists view the artistic process and the place of art in their own lives.*

Chapter 10: From Seeing to Art

- ACTION: *Have children begin to discover what is beautiful inside the classroom as well as what is outside the classroom.*

- ACTION: *Choose an article to sketch, then draw it from different points of view.*

- ACTION: *Use cropping to isolate one part of a larger work.*

- ACTION: *Look for objects or areas that you consider grotesque.*

- ACTION: *Have the children begin to rank various areas in the room according to their aesthetic qualities.*

- ACTION: *Have the children interview a local artist, as I interviewed Juliette Hamelecourt, about the process of art and its connection to their lives.*

122

Chapter 11: Science: Change in Motion

- ACTION: *Consider the changes going on around you.*
- ACTION: *Observe and record the shifts in light and shadow on the floor of a room.*
- ACTION: *Observe an animal or a pet for a period of twenty minutes on two separate occasions.*
- ACTION: *Interview a scientist to discover how he or she thinks.*

Chapter 12: Learning to Think Through Science

- ACTION: *Make a list of things that move right in the classroom.*
- ACTION: *Chart the motion of the sun on paper.*
- ACTION: *Choose a plot of land to examine regularly throughout the school year.*
- ACTION: *Purchase two pumpkins in early September (preferably green) and observe the change in color (green to orange) through to final decay.*
- ACTION: *Observe a pet or any animal over time.*
- ACTION: *Consider a study of fall leaves.*
- ACTION: *Demonstrate to children through a "think-aloud" how you will consider writing up the data about leaves.*
- ACTION: *Interview a scientist.*

References

Becker, Carl L. 1958. *The Declaration of Independence.* New York: Vintage.

Bruner, Jerome. 1990. *Acts of Meaning.* Cambridge, MA: Harvard University Press.

Burns, Ken. 1990. Commencement address, University of New Hampshire, Durham, NH, December.

Carroll, James. 1996. "The Story of Abraham." In *Genesis,* edited by David Rosenberg. San Francisco: Harper.

Cary, Stephen. Forthcoming. *How to Help English Learners.* Portsmouth, NH: Heinemann.

Csikszentmihalyi, Mihaly. 1990. *Flow: The Psychology of Optimal Experience.* New York: Harper & Row.

Dryden, Kenneth. 1983. *The Game.* Toronto: Totem.

Eldredge, Charles C. 1993. *Georgia O'Keeffe: American and Modern.* New Haven: Yale University Press.

Ellis, Joseph. 1997. *American Sphinx: The Character of Thomas Jefferson.* New York: Alfred A. Knopf.

Ernst, Karen. 1994. *Picturing Learning: Artists and Writers in the Classroom.* Portsmouth, NH: Heinemann.

Fabre, Jean-Henri. 1949. *The Insect World of Jean Henri Fabre.* New York: Dodd Mead and Co.

———. 1979. *Insects.* Twickenham, UK: The Felix Gluck Press Ltd.

Fitzgerald, John D. 1973. *The Great Brain Reforms.* New York: Dell.

Fletcher, Ralph. 1997. *Spider Boy.* New York: Clarion Books.

Gardiner, John. 1980. *Stone Fox.* New York: Harper & Row.

George, Jean Craighead. 1987. *Water Sky*. New York: Harpercrest.

Getzels, Jacob, and Mihaly Csikszentimihalyi. 1976. *The Creative Vision: A Longitudinal Study of Problem Finding in Art*. New York: John Wiley and Sons.

Graves, Donald H. 1989. *Experiment with Fiction*. Portsmouth, NH: Heinemann.

———. 1989. *Investigate Nonfiction*. Portsmouth, NH: Heinemann.

———. 1991. *Build a Literate Classroom*. Portsmouth, NH: Heinemann.

———. 1994. *A Fresh Look at Writing*. Portsmouth, NH: Heinemann.

———. 1996. "The Writer–Scientist." *Dragonfly* (April).

Hakim, Joy, ed. 1995. *History of the United States* series. New York: Oxford University Press.

Hassrick, Peter H., ed. 1997. *The Georgia O'Keeffe Museum*. New York: Harry N. Abrams.

Heathcote, Dorothy, and Gavin Bolton. 1995. *Drama for Learning: Dorothy Heathcote's Mantle of the Expert Approach to Education*. Portsmouth, NH: Heinemann.

Hjerter, Kathleen G., ed. 1986. *Doubly Gifted: The Author as Visual Artist*. New York: Harry N. Abrams.

John-Steiner, Vera. 1985. *Notebooks of the Mind: Explorations of Thinking*. Albuquerque: University of New Mexico Press.

Lisle, Laurie. 1986. *Portrait of an Artist: Georgia O'Keeffe*. New York: Washington Square Press.

Mapp, Alfred J. Jr. 1987. *Thomas Jefferson: A Case of Mistaken Identity*. New York: Madison Books.

Mayo, Bernard, ed. 1942. *Jefferson Himself*. Charlottsville: University of Virginia Press.

Meyer, Ralph, and Steven Sheehan. 1991. *The Artist's Handbook of Materials and Techniques*. New York: Viking.

Murray, Donald. 1990. *Shoptalk*. Portsmouth, NH: Boynton/Cook.

National Center for History in Schools. 1996. The National Standards for History.

Patterson, Freeman. 1989. *Photography and the Art of Seeing*. Toronto: Key Porter Books.

Percoco, James. 1998. *A Passion for the Past*. Portsmouth, NH: Heinemann.

Rogovin, Paula. 1998. *Classroom Interviews in Action*. Portsmouth, NH: Heinemann.

Simon, Neil. 1992. "The Art of the Theatre." *Paris Review* 125 (Winter).

Taylor, Philip. 1998. *Redcoats and Patriots: Reflective Practice in Drama and Social Studies*. Portsmouth, NH: Heinemann.

Thomas, Lewis. 1983. *Late Night Thoughts on Mahler's Ninth Symphony*. New York: Viking.

Ulrich, Laurel Thatcher. 1991. *A Midwife's Tale: The Life of Martha Ballard, Based on Her Diary, 1785–1812*. New York: Vintage.

Wagner, B. J. 1998. *Educational Drama and Language Arts: What Research Shows*. Portsmouth, NH: Heinemann.

Wells, Gordon. 1986. *The Meaning Makers: Children Learning Language and Using Language to Learn*. Portsmouth, NH: Heinemann.

Vygotsky, Lev. 1962. *Thought and Language*. Cambridge, MA: MIT Press.

Yekimov, Boris. 1989. "A Greeting from Afar." In *The Human Experience: Contemporary American and Soviet Fiction and Poetry*, edited by the Soviet/American Joint Editorial Board of the Quaker/US/USSR Committee. New York: Alfred A. Knopf; Moscow: Khudozhestvennaya Literatura.